The Story of an Untold Love

Paul Leicester Ford

Alpha Editions

This edition published in 2024

ISBN : 9789362922670

Design and Setting By
Alpha Editions
www.alphaedis.com
Email - info@alphaedis.com

I

February 20, 1890. There is not a moment of my life that you have shared with me which I cannot recall with a distinctness fairly sunlit. My joys and my sorrows, my triumphs and my failures, have faded one by one from emotions into memories, quickening neither pulse nor thought when they recur to me, while you alone can set both throbbing. And though for years I have known that if you enshrined any one in your heart it would be some one worthier of you, yet I have loved you truly, and whatever I have been in all else, in that one thing, at least, I have been strong. Nor would I part with my tenderness for you, even though it has robbed me of contentment; for all the pleasures of which I can dream cannot equal the happiness of loving you. To God I owe life, and you, Maizie, have filled that life with love; and to both I bow my spirit in thanks, striving not to waste his gift lest I be unworthy of the devotion I feel for you.

If I were a stronger man, I should not now be sobbing out my heart's blood through the tip of a pen. Instead of writing of my sorrow, I should have battled for my love despite all obstacles. But I am no Alexander to cut the knot of entanglements which the fates have woven about me, and so, Midas-like, I sit morbidly whispering the hidden grief, too great for me to bear in silence longer.

I can picture my first glimpse of you as vividly as my last. That dull rainy day of indoor imprisonment seems almost to have been arranged as a shadowbox to intensify the image graved so deeply on my memory. The sun came, as you did, towards the end of the afternoon, as if light and warmth were your couriers. When I shyly entered the library in answer to my father's call, you were standing in the full sunlight, and the thought flashed through my mind that here was one of the angels of whom I had read. You were only a child of seven,—to others, I suppose, immature and formless; yet even then your eyes were as large and as serious as they are to-day, and your curling brown hair had already a touch of fire, as if sunshine had crept thereinto, and, liking its abiding-place, had lingered lovingly.

"Don," cried my father, as I stood hesitating in the doorway, "here's a new plaything for you. Give it a welcome and a kiss."

I hung back, half in shyness, and half in fear that you were of heaven, and not of earth, but you came forward and kissed me without the slightest hesitation. The details are so clear that I remember you hardly had to raise your head, though I was three years the older. Your kiss dispelled all my timidity, and from the moment of that caress I loved you. Not that I am so foolish as to believe I then felt for you what now I feel, but by the clear light of retrospect I can see that your coming brought a new element into my life,—an element which I loved from the first, though with steadily deepening intensity, and I cannot even now determine at what point a boy's devotion became a lover's.

To the silent and lonely lad you were an inspiration. What I might have grown to be had you not been my father's ward I do not like to think, for I was not a strong boy, and my shyness and timidity had prompted me to much solitude and few friends, to much reading and to little play. But it was decreed that you were to be the controlling influence of my life, and in the first week you worked a revolution in my habits. I wonder if now, when you see so many men eager to gratify your slightest wish, you ever think of your earliest slave, whom you enticed to the roof to drop pebbles or water on the passers-by, and into the cellar to bury a toy soldier deep in the coal? Does memory ever bring back to you how we started to paint the illustrations in Kingsborough's Mexican Antiquities, or how we built a fire round a doll on the library rug, in imitation of the death of an Inca of Peru as pictured in dear old Garcilasso de la Vega's Royal Commentaries? You were a lazy child about reading, but when not tempting me into riotous mischief, you would sit by me in the library and let me show you the pictures in the old books, and I smile now to think what my running versions of the texts must have been. Our favorite books were the Nuremberg Chronicle and De Bry's Voyages, for the pictures of which, since the Latin was beyond me, I invented explanations and even whole stories,—stories over which you grew big-eyed and sleepless, and which we both came to believe so firmly that we never dreamed them to be the cause for the occasional outburst of laughter from my father, when he was in the library.

Even in those days you veiled your witchery and mischief-loving nature behind that serious face with its curved but unsmiling mouth. Keen as many of our pleasures were and blithe as were our pranks, I can scarcely remember a smile upon your face. Now and then the merriest of laughs rang out, fairly infectious in its happiness and joy, but of so rare recurrence as to win for you the sobriquet of "Madam Gravity." Your inscrutability allured and charmed me then as I have seen it fascinate others since. I shall never understand you, and yet I think I misunderstand you less than others do, for you cannot hide from me the quick thought and merry nature which you keep so well hidden from them; and often when others think you most abstracted or sedate, I know you are holding high carnival with Puck and Momus. Again and again I have noted your gravity in the most humorous situations or with the most ridiculous of persons, and have smiled in secret with you. Last summer, when my mother won such a laugh by telling, as something that had happened to her personally, the old story from Peele's "Merrie Conceits" which we had read as children, you looked grave, though the incident had twice the humor to you that it had to the others. In my own merriment I could not help glancing at you, and though neither of us laughed, we understood each other's amusement. Evidently you were not used to having your mood comprehended, for after a moment you seemed to realize that I was responding to what you had thought unknown to all. You looked startled and then puzzled, and I suppose that I became even more of a mystery to you than ever. You could not know that my knowledge of you came from those early days when your nature was taking shape. Without my memory of you as a child you would be as great an enigma to me as to the rest of your friends, and so no doubt it is a small thing in which to glory. But it gives me joy to feel that I understand you better, and at this very moment know more of your thoughts than your husband ever will.

I owe to you many dark closetings and whippings that I never deserved. My mother complained that from being a troublesome child I had become a fiend of mischief, but my father laughed and predicted that you would make a man of me. I wonder if you ever think of him, and what your thought is? We both so loved him that I cannot believe he has passed entirely out of your heart. How ready he was to be our comrade! Whether tired or busy he would join us, not as mentor but as playfellow; and now that I know what there was to depress his spirits at that time, I marvel at his cheer and courage. Would that I had one half of the bravery with which he met his troubles!

Perhaps he was right in his assumption that you would have made a man of me. I do not recollect any act of mine which bore the semblance of courage except the rescue of the street dog from those boys. I hated to see the poor beast tortured, but I feared the roughs, and so stood faltering while you charged among them. Not till one of them struck you was I driven to help, but I can still feel the fury which then took possession of me. I was blind with rage, and a great weight seemed pressing on my chest as I rushed among the boys and fought, hardly conscious of the blows I gave or received; indeed, the whole thing was a haze until I found myself sitting on the sidewalk, crying. For days I went about with a bandage over my eye; but my father drank my health that night, and I remember his pat of approval, and hear his "Bravo, Donald, I'm proud of you." It was significant that I received all the praise, and you none; my courage was questionable, yours was not.

Those happy, thoughtless years! The one kill-joy was my mother, and she made your life and mine so grievous with her needless harshness, quick temper, and neglect of our comfort that I think she must have made my father's equally miserable. Dimly I can recollect her sudden gusts of temper, and his instant dismissal of us from the room when they began. Do you remember how he used to come up to the nursery to smoke, often staying till our bedtime, and then how we could hear him go downstairs and out of the front door? We did not know that he went to his club, nor at what hour he returned; and if we had it would have meant nothing to us. But we both knew he found no pleasure with my mother, and we felt he was right, for in avoiding her he was but doing what was our chief endeavor. I have heard many express admiration for her beauty, for her church and charitable work, for her brilliancy in society, for her executive ability, and for her general public spirit. Her neglect of family duties, her extravagance, her frequent absences, and her fatigued petulance when at home were known only to her household. Our servants rarely remained a month with us,—were changed so often as to destroy all possibility of comfort; but we three were not free to follow their example, and so our misery made us the dearer to one another. I am proud to think that, close as we drew together, my father never uttered in my presence a single word of criticism or complaint against my mother, and I should be the better man if, instead of writing these unfilial words, I left them unsaid. Indeed, I will not spend more of my evening on these old memories, but begin on my work.

Do you remember, Maizie, how my father taught us to give him and each other a parting word? "Good-night, father. Good-night, Maizie. God bless you both," it used to be. He sleeps now in his grave, and three years ago you barred your door to me, but still I can say as of old, "Good-night, Maizie. God bless and keep you, dear."

II

February 21. To put all this on paper is weak and aimless, yet it seems to ease my sadness. I suppose a scribbler unconsciously comes to write out whatever he feels, as a nervous woman plays her emotions away on a piano. If this is so, why should not I salve my grief in any way that lessens it? Those old days had such happiness in them that the mere memory brings some to me, and to sit here at my study table and write of the past is better than idle dwelling on the present.

You were jubilant when first told that we were all to go to Europe for a summer, and laughed at my fears and despondency. Could I have had an intuition of coming evil, or was my alarm due to the engravings of those terrible sea-monsters with which Mercator populated the oceans in his "Atlas sive Cosmographicæ," and to the pictures and tales in bloodthirsty old Exquemelin's "Bucaniers of America"? Our notions of what the trip meant were evidently not very clear, for at once we set to storing up provisions, and weeks before the time of sailing we were the proud possessors of a cracker-box full of assorted edibles, a jar of olives we had pilfered, and a small pie you had cajoled the cook into making for us. How we loved and gloated over that pie! Daily we sorted our sea-stores, added new supplies, and ate what clearly could be kept no longer. My mother found us one day deeply engrossed in the occupation, cuffed us both, and sent the olives back to the pantry and the tin box to the ash-barrel. As for the pie, such hot words passed about it between "Madame" and "Monsieur Philippe" that our cook left us without warning. We were again punished for being the cause of his desertion, and that evening father dined at his club.

The different effects my mother's gusts of anger had on you and on me were curiously distinctive. You met them fearlessly and stubbornly, while to me the moments of her fury were moments in which I could scarcely breathe, and of which I felt the terror for hours after. I sometimes wonder if the variance was because I had learned to fear the outbursts even as a baby, whereas your character had partly formed before you encountered them. Who knows but a change of circumstances might have made me the fearless one, and you the timorous? At least I should be glad to think that I might have been like you in courage and spirit, even though it is impossible to imagine that you could ever be like me. It is a singular turn of life's whirligig that when my mother tried to pain you last autumn by her cruel remarks, you were helpless to retort, and owed your escape to my help.

What a delight the ocean voyage was to us! Those were the times of ten-day trips, still dear to all true lovers of the sea; and had our wishes been consulted, thrice ten would have been none too long for our passage. The officers, the crew, the stewards, and the passengers were no more proof against your indefinable spell than was I, and it seemed quite as if the boat were your private yacht, with all on board seeking only to serve you. Our pleasure was so intense that we planned an ideal future, in which I was to become the captain of a steam-ship, and you were to live on the vessel in some equally delightful if impossible capacity.

The last time I was in Paris, I walked several miles merely to look at the outside of our pension, and then went on and sat dreaming in the little park near it in which we passed so many hours of our stay in that city. As of old, the place was full of children and nurses, and I understood what had puzzled me not a little in recollection,—how you and I, without mingling with them, had learned so quickly the language they chattered. Do you remember their friendly advances, met only by rebuffs? My coldness flowed from shyness, and yours from a trait that people to this day call haughtiness, but which I know to be only a fastidious refinement that yields acquaintance to few and friendship to fewer. From the moment you came into my life I craved no other friend, and you seemed equally content. What was there in me that won for me what you gave so rarely? Was there an instinct of natural sympathy, or was it merely pity for me in the loving heart you masked behind that subtle face?

It is indicative of what children we still were that during the whole of our sojourn in Paris neither of us was conscious that our standard of living had changed. We lodged in a cheap pension; instead of our own carriage we used the omnibus; and a thousand other evidences told the story of real economy; yet not one we observed except the disappearance of our *bonne*, and this was noted, not as a loss, but as a joy to both.

After the nurse was gone my father became more than ever our comrade, and a better one two children never had. Oh, those long excursions to Versailles, Montmartre, and Fontainebleau, our boat trips up and down the Seine, and our shorter jaunts within the city! What happiness it was to us when he came in whistling and cried, "Donald, Maizie, you are horribly bad children, and I'm going to take you on a lark to punish you!" After time spent in filling our lunch-basket with big rolls bought at the *boulangerie*, a few sous' worth of cherries or other fruit lengthily bargained for with the *fruitier*, and a half litre of cheap wine, plus whatever other luxuries our imaginations or our appetites could suggest, away we would go for a long day of pure delight, whether passed under green trees or wandering through galleries and museums. My father was an encyclopædia of information, and had the knack of making knowledge interesting to the child mind. He could re-create a bygone period from a battle-axe or a *martel de fer*, the personality of a queen from her lace ruff or stomacher, and the history of plant growth from a fern or flower. If his mind had been allowed to expand when he was young, instead of being stunted in a broker's office, I believe he might have been one of the world's great writers or critics.

Under such stimulating tutelage our progress in those two years was really wonderful. No subject my father touched upon could remain dull; we were at a receptive age when the mind is fresh and elastic for all that interests it, and Paris was a great picture-book to illustrate what he taught us. We did not know we were studying far deeper into subjects than many educated people ever go. I laugh still at your telling the old German on the train to Sèvres the history of the Faust plot, and at his amazed "Ach, zo!" to hear such erudition pour from your childish lips. I think you were the cleverer and the quicker, but there was no competition, only fellowship about our learning. I suppose you were above rivalry, as you are above all mean things.

And that is your chief glory to me. In those seven years of closest companionship, and in these last three years of lesser intercourse but far keener observation, I have never known you to do a mean thing or to speak a mean thought. I almost feel it treason to couple the word with you, or deny a trait so impossible for you to possess, and of which you have always shown such scorn and hatred. At this moment I know that I should only have to speak to part you forever from—Ah, what foolishness I am writing, tempting me to even greater meanness than his, and so to deserve the greater contempt from you! Thinking me base, you closed your doors to me three years ago, and I love you the better that not even for auld lang syne could you pardon what is so alien to you. If the day ever comes when you again admit me to your friendship, I shall be happy in knowing that you think me above baseness or meanness; for you would not compound with them, Maizie, be the circumstances what they might.

Our Paris life would not have been so happy and careless but for the slight part my mother had in it. So little did we see of her in those years that I think of her scarcely as one of us. I remember dimly a scene of hot anger between her and my father,—he standing passively by the high porcelain stove, while she raged about the room. So great was her fury that once, in passing, as I crouched scared and silent on the sofa, she struck me,—a blow which brought my father to my side, where he stood protectingly while the storm lasted, with his hand resting lovingly on my shoulder. My vague impression is that the outburst was only a protest against the poor lodgings, but it may have occurred when some explanation took place between my parents. I can see my mother now, sitting on the little balcony overlooking the garden of our pension, snarling an ill-natured word at us as you and I tried to play consultation games of chess against my father. He gave us odds at first of the rook and two pawns, but finally only of a knight. Oh, the triumph of those victories! How we gloried in them, and how delighted our antagonist was when we conquered him! Little we minded what my mother did except when we happened to be alone with her, and I think that the dear father played bad chess with us rather than good at the cafés, and made us his companions wherever he went, to save us from her severity.

I can recall very clearly her constant difficulties with our landlady and the servants, which finally culminated in a request that we should seek lodgings elsewhere. Do you recollect Madame Vanott's clasping us both in her arms and filling our hands with bonbons, when the time of parting came? I do not know where we removed to, my sole remembrance of the next few weeks being of my mother's complaints of lodgings, food, servants, and French life generally. We moved three times within a month, fairly expelled by our landlords because they could not live at peace with "la Madame." Our last exodus began in an angry scene between her and the housewife, in which a gendarme played a part, and from which you and I fled. The next morning we learned that my mother had determined to return to America, and leave us to live our own life. Three days later we said emotionless good-bys, my father going as far as Havre with her.

Her departure set us asking questions, and my father's replies explained many things which, in our childish talks, we had gravely discussed. He told us how his own wealth had been lost in Wall Street, barely enough being left for a competence even in Europe. Of my mother's leaving us he spoke sadly. "She never pretended to care for me," he said, "but I loved her and was willing to marry her. The wrong was mine, and we should not blame her if, when I can no longer give what was her price, she does not choose to continue the one-sided bargain." At the time her absence seemed to you and me only a relief, but now, as I look back, I know that my father never ceased to love her,—all the more, perhaps, because his love had never been requited,—and that separation must have been the final wrecking of his life. Yet from the day she left us I never heard him speak an angry word, and sorrow that would have crushed most men seemed to make him the gentler and sweeter. I wish—Ah! the clock is striking three, and if I am to bring working power to working hours I must stop writing.

Good-night, dear one.

III

February 22. After my mother left us we did not stay in Paris, but went to Ischl, which we made merely the point of departure for walking tours which often lasted for weeks. Several times I have spoken of the region to you, hoping to draw from you some remark proving a recollection of those days, but you always avoid reply. Yet I am sure they are not forgotten, for miles of the Tyrol and Alps are as familiar to me as the garnishings of a breakfast-table. My father had the tact and kindly humor that make a man equally at home and welcome in *Gasthaus* and *Schloss*. Though we traveled with only a knapsack, his breeding and education were so patent to whomsoever we met that we spent many a night inside of doors with armorial coats of many quarterings carved above them, and many a day's shooting and fishing followed. Yet pleasant as was this impromptu and "gentle" hospitality, I think we were all quite as happy when our evenings were spent among the peasants, drinking beer, talking of farming and forestry, singing songs, or listening to the blare of the peripatetic military band.

My father was a fine German scholar, and you and I acquired the language as quickly and as easily as we learned French. We always had books in our pockets, and used to lie for hours under the trees, reading aloud. Long discussions followed over what we had conned, enriched by the thousand side-lights my father could throw on any subject. To most people reading is a resort to save themselves from thinking, but my father knew that pitfall, and made us use books as a basis for thought on our own part. After a volume was finished we would each write a criticism of it, and the comparison of my boyish attempts with his brilliant, comprehensive, and philosophic work taught me more of writing than all the tuition I ever had.

My craving for knowledge, always strong, became inordinate, probably because the acquisition of it was made so fascinating that I learned without real exertion. I began to find limits even to my father's erudition, and chafed under them. He reviewed his Greek that he might impart it to us, as he had long before taught us Latin, and together we all three studied Spanish and Italian. I was not satisfied, for my desire for the one thing my father was unable to teach was not appeased by the twenty which he could. I begged for regular tuition, and, indulgent as he always was, he took us to Heidelberg, where I was enrolled in the gymnasium. Yet the long hours of separation that this entailed made little difference in our relations, since except for these we were inseparable. Whenever my school-work left us time to quit Heidelberg we made walking tours, and we availed ourselves of the summer holiday to see far-away lands. The great libraries were our chief goals, but everything interested us, from the archaic plough we saw in the field to the masterpiece of the gallery. I do not know whether I was dull for my years, but I do know that you were precocious and had no difficulty in keeping up with me in my studies. Indeed, thanks to your own brightness and to the long hours spent with my father while I was reciting, you went ahead of me in many respects. It makes me very happy now to think of what you two were to each other, and to know that you are so largely indebted to him for the depth and brilliance of mind that I hear so often commented upon. And I love you all the better because you made those years so happy to him by your love and companionship.

Last winter Mrs. Blodgett accused me of being a misogynist, and proved her point by asking me to tell the color of Agnes's eyes. You and Agnes only laughed when I miscolored them, but Mrs. Blodgett was really nettled. "There!" she said. "Apparently, Agnes and I are the only women you ever go to see or pretend to care for, and yet you think so little of us that you don't know the color of our eyes." Had she only asked me to describe your eyes in place of Agnes's I should not have erred, but I suppose even then the world would be justified in thinking I do not care for woman's society. Certainly you, of all others, have the right to think so, after my twice refusing your friendship; and yet it is my love of you far more than my studies or shyness that has made me indifferent to other women. And so far from being a misogynist, I care for as few men as women. You perhaps recall how much apart I kept myself from my fellow students, and how my father had to urge me to join them in the fencing and chess contests? Later, at the university, after you had left us, I entered more eagerly into the two pastimes, and succeeded in making myself a skilled swordsman. As for chess, I learned to play the game you tested last October on the veranda of My Fancy. You looked courteously grave when, after our initial battle, I had to ask from you the odds of a pawn, and never dreamed that I fathomed your secret triumph over your victory. You are so delightfully human and womanly, after all, Maizie, to any one who can read your thoughts. It is a pleasure to see your happiness in the consciousness of your own power, and I grudge you victory over me no more than over other men. Yet while you play better chess, I think you could not conquer me quite as easily if I were not much more interested in studying the player than the play. Perhaps but for you I should have made friends, for later, at Leipzig, despite my shyness and studiousness, I seemed fairly popular; but so long as I had you I cared for no other friend, and after our separation I could form no new tie. Neither in love nor in friendship have you ever had a rival in my heart.

Our happiness ended the day when Johann, the poor factotum of our lodging-place, found us in the castle park and summoned us back to the house, where my father and Mr. Walton were awaiting you. The news that we were to be parted came so suddenly that we could not believe it. I stood in stunned silence, while you declared that you would not go with your uncle; even in that terrible moment speaking more like a queen issuing orders than like a rebel resisting authority. We both appealed to my father, and the tears stood in his eyes as he told us we must be parted. Mr. Walton sat with the cool and slightly bored look that his worldly face wears so constantly, and I presume it was impossible for him to understand our emotion.

Your luggage had been packed while we were being summoned, and I carried your bag down to the carriage, in the endeavor to do you some last little service. We did not even go through the form of a farewell, but, tearless and speechless, held each other's hands till my father gently separated us. To this day the snap of a whip causes me to catch my breath, it brings back so vividly the crack with which Mr. Walton's cabman whipped up his horse. Fate was merciful, for she gave me no glimpse of the future, and so left me the hope that we should not be parted long. I question if the delicate lad of those days could have borne the thought that our separation, enforced by others, would in time be continued by you.

The life was too happy to last; and yet I do not know why I write that, for I do not believe that God's children are born to be wretched, and I would sooner renounce my faith in him than believe him so cruel to his own creations. The sadness and estrangement in my life are all of human origin, and mine, it seems to me, has been a fuller cup of bitterness than most men have to drink. Or am I only magnifying my own sufferings, and diminishing those of my fellow mortals? To the world I am a fortunate man, with promise of even greater success. Do all the people about me, who seem to be equally prosperous, bury away from sight some grief like mine that beggars joy?

Can you, Maizie, in the tide and triumph of your beauty and wealth, hide any such death-wound to all true happiness? Pray God you do not. Good-night, my darling.

IV

February 23. After you were gone I fled to my room, crawling under the window-seat, much as a mortally wounded animal tries to hide itself. Here my father found me many hours later, speechless and shivering. He drew me from my retreat, and I still remember the sting of the brandy as he poured it down my throat. Afterwards the doctor came, to do nothing; but all that night my father sat beside me, and towards morning he broke down my silence, and we talked together over the light which had gone out of our lives, till I fell asleep. He told me that the death of your two aunts had made you a great heiress, and rendered your continuance with us, in our poverty, impossible. "She's gone away out of our class, Donald," my father said sadly, "and in the change of circumstances her mother wouldn't have made me her guardian. It was better for all of us to let her uncle take her back to New York." Even in my own grief I felt his sorrow, and though he did not dodge my questions, I could see how the subject pained him, and avoided it thenceforth. How strangely altered my life would have been if I had insisted on knowing more!

The doctor came several times afterwards, for I did not rally as I should have done, and at last he ordered a year's cessation of studies and plenty of exercise. It was a terrible blow to me at the time, for I was on the point of entering the University of Leipzig; but now I can see it was all for the best, since the time given to our tours through Spain and Italy was well spent, and the delay made me better able to get the full value of the lectures. Moreover, that outdoor life added three inches to the height and seventeen pounds to the weight of the hitherto puny boy. For a time my father made my health his care, and insisted on my walking and fencing daily; but after that long holiday he need not have given it a thought, for I grew steadily to my present height, and while always of slender build, I can outwalk or outwork many a stockier man.

My university career was successful; it could hardly have failed to be, with my training. I fear that I became over-elated with my success, not appreciating how much it was due to my father's aid and to the kindness of two of my instructors. For my Ph. D. I made a study of the great race movements of the world, in which my predilection for philology, ethnology, and history gave me an especial interest. I so delighted my professor of philology by my enthusiasm and tirelessness that he stole long hours from the darling of his heart to aid me. (I need hardly add that I do not allude to Frau Jastrow, but to his Verb-Roots of Fifty-Two Languages and Dialects of Indo-Germanic Origin, to be published some day in seventeen volumes, quarto.) He even brought me bundles of his manuscript to read and criticise. Our relations were as intimate as were possible between a professor and a student, and despite his reputation for ill temper the only evidence he ever gave me of it was a certain querulousness over the gaps in human knowledge.

My doctor's thesis on A Study of the Influence of Religion in the Alienation and Mixture of Races—which, with a vanity I now laugh over, I submitted not merely in Latin, but as an original work in four other languages—was not only the delight of both my dear professors, but was well considered outside the university. At Jastrow's urging, poor Buchholtz printed editions in all five languages; and as only the German had any sale worth mentioning, he ever after looked gloomy at a mere allusion to the title. But though it earned me no royalties, it won me the Kellermann prize, given every fifth year for the best original work on an historical subject.

On our first arrival in Leipzig my father sought literary employment from the great publishers of that city of books, and soon obtained all the "review" and "hack" writing that he wished. He encouraged me to help him in the work, and in my training probably lay his chief inducement, for he was paid at starvation rates in that land of hungry authors. The labor quickly taught me the technical part of authorship, the rock which has wrecked so many hopes. Our work brought us, too, the acquaintance of many literary men, and thus gave us our pleasantest society, and one peculiarly fitted to develop me. Furthermore, we secured command of the unlimited books stored on the publishers' shelves, which we used as freely as if they were our own private library.

Very quickly I began to do more than help my father in his work; I myself tried to write. He put many a manuscript in the fire, after going over the faults with me, but finally I wrote something that he let me send to an editor. His admirable judgment must have been warped by his fatherly love, for the article was rejected. A like fate befell many others, but at last one was accepted, and I do not know which of us was the more delighted when it was published in the "Zeitschrift für Deutsche Philologie." By my father's advice it was signed with a pseudonym; for he pointed out that I was still too young for editors who knew me to give my manuscript a reading, and that a German name would command greater respect from them than an English one.

I received twenty marks for that first article, and spent it in secret the next day. Had you known of my pleasure in the gift, and the hopes that went with it, I think you would have sent a line of acknowledgment to the hungry-hearted fellow who, after four years of separation, still longed for a token from you. Three times had I written, without response, but I thought the beauty of the photograph would so appeal to you that it must bring me back a word from you, and lived in the hope for six months. My father joked me genially about what I had done with that vast wealth, pretending at moments that he believed it had been avariciously hoarded, and at other times that it had been squandered in riotous living, till one day, when all hope of acknowledgment had died, his chaff wrung from me an exclamation of pain, suppressed too late to be concealed from him. So closely attuned had we become that he understood in an instant what it meant, and, laying his hand on my shoulder, he appealed, "Forgive me, my boy! I have been very cruel in my thoughtlessness!"

Nothing more was said then, but later that evening, when we rose from our work, he asked, "She never replied?" and when I shook my head, the saddest look I ever saw in him came upon his face. He seemed about to speak impulsively, faltered, checked himself, and finally entreated, "Bear up, Donald, and try to forget her." I could only shake my head again, but he understood. "She's feminine quicksilver," he groaned, "and I can't get the dear girl out of my blood, either." We gripped each other's hands for a moment, and I said, "Good-night, father," and he replied, "God help you, my boy." How happy we should have been could we have bidden you, "Good-night, Maizie!"

V

February 24. I cannot clearly fix the time when first I decided upon a life of letters, and presume it was my father's influence which determined me. After the publication of my first article, all the time I could spare from my studies was devoted to writing. Most of it was magazine work, but two text-books were more ambitious flights. Undertaken at my father's suggestion, the books were revised by him, till they should have been published with his name, and not my pseudonym, on the title-page. This I urged, but he would not hear of it, insisting that his work was trivial compared with mine. I understand his motive now, and see how wise and loving he was in all his plans. Thanks to his skill in clarifying knowledge and fitting it to the immature mind, both books attained a large sale almost immediately on their publication.

My father's abnegation went further, and occasioned the only quarrel we ever had. After the publication of several of my articles, in reading the Deutsche Rundschau I found an interesting critique signed with the name I had adopted as a pseudonym. I laughingly called my father's attention to it, yet really feeling a little sore that the credit of my work should go to another, for the first literary offspring are very dear to an author's heart. From that time I was constantly meeting with the name, but stupidly failed to recognize my father's brilliant, luminous touch till the publication of another article of my writing revealed the truth to me; for at the end of this I found again my pseudonym, though I had signed my own name. On my sending an indignant letter to the editor, he returned me the revised proof of my article, at the bottom of which "Donald Maitland" was struck out, and "Rudolph Hartzmann" substituted. My father had made the change in the last revision, and had returned the sheets without letting me see them.

In a moment the veil was gone from my eyes, and, grieved and angry, I charged him with the deception. I do not like to think of what I said or of the gentleness with which he took it. The next day, when I was cooler, he pleaded with me to let him continue signing the name to his articles; but I insisted that I would not permit the double use, and the only concession he could win from me was that I would still keep the name provided he refrained from using it again. How could I resist his "Don, I never asked anything but this of you. I am an old man with no possibility of a career. You are all I have to love or work for in this world. Let me try to help you gain a name." Oh, father, if I had only understood, I would not have been so cruel as to deny your request, but would have sacrificed my own honesty and allowed the lie rather than have refused what now I know to have been so dear a wish. I even resented what I thought a foolish joke of his, when he registered us constantly at hotels as "Rudolph Hartzmann and father." It is poetic justice that in time I should stoop to so much greater dishonesty than that which I was intolerant of in him.

Owing as much to his articles as to those I subsequently wrote, my pseudonym became a recognized one in the world of letters, and my work soon commanded a good price. Furthermore, considerable interest was excited as to the author. There is a keen delight in anonymous publication, for one does not get the one-sided chatter that acknowledged authors receive, and often I have sat in the midst of a group of littérateurs and scholars and heard my articles talked over. I was tempted even to discuss one,—disparaging it, of course,—and can remember the way my father hid his laughter when a member of the party said, "Maitland, you ought to write an article refuting Hartzmann, for you've got the knowledge to do it." It amuses me to think how vain and elated I became over what now I see was only 'prentice work. I am glad you did not know me in those years of petty victory, and that before we met I had been saddened and humbled.

Some one at Mr. Whitely's dinner, this winter, asked what was a sufficient income, and you, Maizie, gravely answered, "A little more than one has," which made us all laugh. If you had not been the quicker and the wittier, and thus forestalled me, I should have said, "Enough to satisfy the few or many wishes each person creates within himself which money can satisfy." Thanks to my prize, my writings, and the profits of my text-books, I obtained this. In fact, the three so lengthened my purse that I fancy few millionaires have ever felt so truly rich; for I was enabled to gratify my greatest wish. In our visits to Spain, Italy, and Constantinople, I had garnered all that I could find bearing on the two great race movements of the Moors and Turks, which so changed the world's history; but I had discovered that I needed more than the documentary materials to write clearly of them. I longed to go to their source, and then follow the channels along which those racial floods had rushed, till, encountering the steel armor and gunpowder of Europe, they had dashed in scattered spray, never to gather force again. In my eagerness I had been for making the attempt before, but my father had urged our limited means and the shortness of my university vacations as bars to my wishes. My degree removed the one objection, and my earnings and prize the other. Few persons would care to undertake the travel we planned with the pittance we had earned, but it was enough for us. How fortunate it is for me that my student life and travels trained me to absolute self-denial and frugality! Otherwise these last three years of closest economy and niggardliness would have been hard to bear.

By the influence of Professor Humzel, working first through his former pupil, Baron Weiseman, secondly through Giers, and thirdly through I know not whom, we secured permission to join a Russian surveying party, and thus safely and expeditiously reached the mountains of the Altai range. We did not stay with the party after they began their work, but assuming native dress we turned southward; plunging instantly among the medley of peoples and tongues which actually realizes the mythical Babel. Turkish, Hebrew, Arabic, and Sanskrit I had mastered in varying degrees, and they were an "open sesame" to the dialects we encountered, while the hot sun and open-air life soon colored us so deeply that we passed for men of a distant but not alien race. Following nature's routes, once man's only paths, we wandered leisurely: to Tashkend on horseback, to Bokhara on foot, by boat down the Amoo to Khiva, and on to Teheran, then by caravan to Bagdad, up the Euphrates, gradually working through Asia Minor. Stopping at Smyrna for a brief rest, we took boat to Cyprus, from thence crossed to Damascus, and from Jerusalem traveled along the caravan route to Mecca. Passing over the Red Sea to Egypt, we skirted the south coast of the Mediterranean, till we reached the Pillars of Hercules.

You ought to have made that pilgrimage. In speaking of my book you expressed the wish that you might make such a trip, and those years would have been as great a playtime to you as to us. You could have borne the exposure, rough though the life was, and it would have been as compound oxygen to your brave and venturesome nature. I confess I do not like to think of that dazzlingly pure skin burned to any such blackness as I saw in my mirror on reaching the end of our journeyings; for truly no better Arab in verisimilitude strolled about the native quarter of Tangier in May, 1886, than Donald Maitland.

My long study of those older races and three years' life spent among them have not made me accept their dogma of fatalism, yet I must believe that something stronger than chance produced our meeting in that Moorish town. Down streams, over mountains, and across deserts, seas, and oceans, our paths had converged; on foot, mounted, by rail or boat, we came together as if some hidden magnet were drawing us both. A thousand chances were against our meeting, even when we were in the same town; for you were housed in the best hotel, while we lodged in a little Jewish place in the Berber quarter. In another day my father and I should have crossed to Spain, without so much as a visit to the European section. But for that meeting I should have returned to Leipzig, and passed a contented life as a Herr Doctor and Professor; for though my heart was still warm with love of you, it had been denied and starved too long to have the strength to draw me from the path my head had marked out.

Yet I would not now accept the unemotional and peaceful career I had planned in lieu of my present life; for if my love is without hope, it is still love, and though you turned me away from your door with far less courtesy than you would shut out a beggar, yet I am near you and see you constantly, and that is worth more to me than peace. Good-night, my love. God bless you.

VI

February 25. It was thought of you which led to our meeting. After the evening meal of dried salt fish, pancakes, dates, and coffee, my father and I wandered out to the Sok, and, as was our wont, sat down among the people. Refusing the hasheesh water and sweetmeats which the venders urged upon us, "to make you dream of your love joyfully," we listened to the story-tellers and the singers. Some one with a fine natural voice sang presently an Arabic love-song:—

> "My love, so lovely yet so cruel,
> Why came you so to torture me?
> Could I but know the being who
> Has caused you thus to hate me!
> Once I saw and gazed upon your lovely form each hour,
> But now you ever shun me.
> Yet still each night you come in dreams
> For me to ask, Who sent you?
> Your answer is, Him whom I love,
> And you bid me then forget my passion.
> But I reply, If it was not for love, how could the world go
> on?"

It was a song I had heard and loved in many lands and many dialects, but that night it stirred me deeply, and brought to mind your image, ever dear. I sat and dreamed of you till the farrago about me became unbearable; and whispering a word to my father, I rose and strode away, with a yearning truly mastering. I could have had no thought that you were near, for when we stood far closer I was still unconscious of your presence. But if not an intuition, I ask what could it be?

Wandering through the narrow streets without purpose or goal, I presently saw looming above me the great hill on which stands the Alcassaba. Climbing in the brilliant moonlight up the steep and ill-conditioned road, and passing that jumble of buildings upon which so many races and generations have left their impress, I strolled along the wall to a ruined embrasure at the corner overlooking the sea. How long I stood there leaning upon the parapet I do not know. Not till you were close upon me was I conscious that my solitude was ended.

I heard footsteps, but was too incurious to turn and glance at the intruders. Nay, more, when that harsh, strident, American voice demanded, "There, isn't that great?" I felt so irritated by both tone and words that but for the seeming rudeness I should have moved away at once. You spoke so low I could not hear your reply, and I wonder what you said,—for his "great" applied to such beauty must have rasped much more on your artistic sense than it did on mine.

"And this black fellow in the turban standing here," continued the strident voice, "he fits, too, like the paper on the wall, though probably he's a sentry taking forty winks on the sly. It makes an American mad to see how slack things are run over here."

I heard a gentle "Hush," and then a murmur as you went on speaking.

"None of these black fellows speak English," came the self-assured voice again. Then, though I could have heard his natural tone full fifty feet away, the man called much louder: "Hey! what's the name of that point out there?"

I should have chosen to make no answer; but remembering the courtesy and dignity of the race I was impersonating, I replied without turning, "Cape Spartel."

You must have said something, for a moment later he laughed, saying, "Not a bit of it. Now see me jolly him up." I heard footsteps, and then some one leaned against the parapet, close beside me. "Backsheesh," he intimated, and jingled some coins in his pocket.

I stood silent, so he tapped me on the shoulder and asked, "Are you one of the palace guards?" Unsuppressed by my monosyllabic "No," he persisted by saying, "What's your business, then?" jingling his coins again. "Stop pulling me, Mai," he added, as an aside.

"I am a stranger in Tangier," I answered quietly.

"From whereabouts?" he questioned.

"The East."

"Oh, you're one of the wise men, are you?" he observed jocosely. "Are you a Jew or a Mohammedan?"

"Not the latter, fortunately for you."

"And why fortunately?" he nagged.

"Because a true believer would have taken the question as a deadly insult."

"They'd be welcome," he laughed, "though it is rather irritating to be mistaken for a Jew. I shouldn't like it myself."

I thought of the dignified Jew traders who had made part of our caravan in the journey from Bagdad to Damascus, and answered, "There is little danger of that."

"I guess not," he assented. "But if you aren't a Jew or a Mohammedan, what are you?"

He had spoiled my mood, and since it was gone I thought I would amuse myself with the man. "A seeker of knowledge from the Altai Mountains," I responded.

"Never heard of them," he announced; "or is it your Choctaw for those?" he added, pointing towards the dark masses of the Atlas Mountains.

I smiled and answered, "They are many moons' travel from here."

"Oh!" he exclaimed. "How did you happen to come?"

"To follow after those gone before."

"I see," he said. "Relatives, I suppose? Hope you found them well?"

"No," I replied, carrying on the humor, "dying."

He jingled his coins, and asked, "Anything to be done for them?"

"Nothing."

"What's the complaint?"

"Civilization in the abstract, repeating rifles and rapid-firing guns in the concrete."

"Eh!" he ejaculated.

Then the lowest and sweetest of voices said, "Won't you tell us what you mean?"

Was it my irritation that the man before me, rather than the subtler-passioned people I knew so well, was the dominant type of the moment, or was it the sympathy your voice stirred within me, which made me speak? In a moment I was sketching broadly the inhumanity of this thing we call Christian civilization, which, more grasping than the Inquisition, has overrun the world, tearing the lands from their owners, and, not content with this spoliation, demands of its victims that they shall give up the customs of many centuries' evolution, and conform to habits, governments, and religions which their very instincts make impossible; and because they cannot change, but break out, these believers in the golden rule shoot them down. I protested at the mockery of calling civilized a world held at peace by constant slaughter, or of styling the national Jack Ketches of humanity Christian nations! I protested against the right of one man to hold another barbaric because he will not welcome his master, greet with joy the bands of steel we call railroads, and crush his nature within the walls of vast factories, to make himself the threefold slave of society, government, and employer. And finally, I gloried in the fact that though the white races had found a weapon against the black and yellow ones which enabled them to overrun and subjugate, yet nature had provided nature's people with the defense of climate,—a death-line to the whites; and behind that line the colored races are unconquerable in the sense of conquest being extinction. I knew the other side, that altruistic tenet of political economy defined in brief as "the greatest good of the greatest number," and in my mind held the even balance of the historian between the two; but to this utilitarian, modern, self-satisfied American I had to urge the rights of races thousands of years our senior, and far in advance of us in the knowledge and amenities that make life worth the most.

You both were silent till I ended; but I had best left unspoken what your companion could not understand, for when I finished he inquired, "What mountains did you say you came from?" And when I told him, he added laughingly, "You must have some pretty good stump speaking in your elections."

"We are very grateful for your explanation," you thanked me gently.

"Never been in America?" he surmised; and except for you I should have told him that I was his countryman, it would have been so adequate a retort to his inference. But your voice and manner had made me so ashamed of my earlier mood that I merely answered, "Yes."

"Humph!" he grunted in surprise; and as if to prove his incorrigibility he continued, "Thought your ideas were too back-number for that."

I could not help laughing, and the moment my laugh became articulate yours too overflowed your lips, as a spring breaks past its edges and falls rippling over pebbles.

That laugh, so well remembered, revealed your presence to me. My heart beat quickly and my head whirled dizzily, and in my bewilderment I took a step backward, quite forgetting the embrasure, till a stone gave way and I felt that I was falling. Then my consciousness went from me, and when thought came surging backward I lay a moment quiet, thinking it must have been a dream.

"He's coming round all right," I heard, and at the sound I opened my eyes. You were leaning over me with the moonlight shining on your face, and I caught my breath, you were so beautiful.

"You've given us a scare," continued the man, on whose knee my head was resting. "You want to keep your wits about you better. Pretty poor business tumbling off walls, but that's what comes of having ruins. You won't be quite so cocky in the future about your run-out races."

I felt his laughter justified, but hardly heeded it, my thoughts were so engaged. You were wetting my forehead with brandy, and I lay there too happy to speak.

"Now let me raise you a bit higher," the man offered kindly, "so you can get your addled senses back." He lifted me, and I groaned at the sudden terrible pain that shot up my leg.

"Hello!" he cried, laying me gently down. "Something wrong, after all? What is it?"

"My leg," I moaned.

"Here, Maizie, hold his head, while I appoint an investigating committee," he ordered, and in another moment I felt your arms about me, and in my joy at your touch I almost forgot my torture.

"Well, you've broken one of your walking-sticks," the man informed me, after a gentler touching of it than I thought possible to his nature. "Now, Maizie, if you'll sit and hold his head, I'll get a litter. You won't mind staying here alone, will you?"

"It is my wish," you acceded calmly.

"O. K.," he said, rising, and even in his kindness he could not help but seize the opportunity to glorify his country. "If this had happened in New York, Mr. Altai, we'd have had an ambulance here five minutes ago! Civilization isn't all bad, I tell you, as you'd find out if you'd give it a chance."

The moment he was gone I tried to speak, and murmured "Maizie;" but you let me get no further, saying "Hush," and putting your hand softly over my lips. I suppose you thought me merely repeating the name he had called you, while I loved your touch too deeply to resist the hand I longed to kiss. Now I am glad I did not speak, for if I had it would have robbed me of my last sweet moment with you.

Long before I thought it possible, and far too soon, indeed, despite my suffering, we heard men approaching. When the torch-bearers came climbing over the rocks, my first desire was to see how much of your beauty was owing to the moonlight, and my heart leaped with exultation to find that you were beautiful even in the livid glare of the torches.

"Now, Mr. Altai," your companion remarked, "where shall we take you?" and I gave him the name of the hotel. A moment later, as they lifted me, I again fainted, but not till I had kissed your hand. You snatched it away, and did not hear my weakly whispered "Good-night, Maizie."

VII

February 26. The setting of my leg, that night, was so long and exhausting an operation that after it was done I was given an opiate. Instead of bringing oblivion the drug produced a dreamy condition, in which I was cognizant of nothing that happened about me, and saw only your face. I knew I ought to sleep, and did my best to think of other things; but try as I might, my thought would return and dwell upon your beauty.

I have often wished I had been born an artist, that I might try to paint your portrait, for words can no more picture you than they can transmit the fragrance of a violet. Indeed, to me the only word which even expresses your charm is "radiant," and that to others, who have never seen you, would suggest little. No real beauty can be described, for it rests in nothing that is tangible. In truth, to speak of your glorious hair, the whiteness of your brow and throat, the brilliant softness of your eyes, or the sweetness yet strength of your tender though unsmiling lips is to make but a travesty of description. I have heard painters talk of your hair and try to convey an idea of its beauty, but I know it too well even to make the attempt. When we were gazing at the rainbow, last autumn, and you said that if its tints could be transferred to a palette you believed it would be possible to paint anything, I could not help correcting, "Except your hair." You laughed, and declared, "I did not know you ever made that kind of a speech!" whereupon Agnes cried, "Didn't I ever tell you, Maizie, the compliment the doctor paid you last winter?" I thought she was alluding to my retort when my mother asserted that your eyes were so large and lustrous that, to her, they were "positively loud." Indignant at such a remark, Agnes had appealed to me to deny it. Not caring to treat the malicious speech seriously, I had answered that I could not agree, though I had sometimes thought your eyes "too dressy for the daytime,"—a joke I have heard so often quoted that it is apparently in a measure descriptive, yet one which I should have felt mortified at hearing repeated to you. Fortunately Agnes's reference was to another remark of mine, in which, speaking of your mouth, I had crudely translated a couple of lines from a Persian poem:—

> "In vain you strive to speak a bitter word—
> It meets the sweetness of your lips ere it is heard."

You were too used to compliments to be embarrassed when the lines were repeated, and only looked at me in a puzzled way. I do not wonder you were surprised at the implied admiration of the two speeches, after my apparent coldness and indifference. My behavior must seem to you as full of contradictions as your beauty is to me. To say your great attraction is the radiance—the verve, spirit, and capacity for enthusiasm—of which one cannot fail to be conscious is to deny the calm dignity with which you bear yourself, yet both these qualities belong to you. The world insists that you are proud and distant, and your face has the clean-cut features which we associate with patrician blood, while your height and figure, and the set and carriage of your head upon that slender throat, suggest a goddess. But I, who understand you so much better than the world, know that your proud face overlies the tenderest of natures, and is not an index, but a mask of feelings you do not care to show. As for the people who criticise you most, they would be the last to do so if they were not conscious of the very superiority they try to lessen.—Ah, how foolish it is to write all this, as if I needed to convince myself of what I know so well! And even if this were for the eye of others, to those who know you not it would be but the extravagant idealism for which a lover is proverbial.

When I awoke from the sleep my dreaming had drifted into, my first request of my father was to find your whereabouts. He told me that a dragoman had come that morning to inquire for me,—and had left what now he showed me,—a great bunch of roses and a basket of fruit, with the card of "Mr. Foster G. Blodgett, 547 Fifth Avenue," on the back of which was written:—

"With sincere regrets that a previously formed plan of leaving Tangier this morning prevents our seeing our courteous instructor of last night, and with hopes that he may have a quick and easy recovery from his accident."

The card was a man's, but the handwriting was feminine, and the moment my father turned his back I kissed it. I was further told that the servant had asked my name and taken it down, giving me the instant hope that when you knew to whom you had been so merciful, you would even disarrange your plans to let me have a moment's glimpse of you. But though I listened all the afternoon hopefully and expectantly, you never came. I felt such shyness about you, I did not speak to my father of your beauty, and he did not question me at all.

Our native hotel, built in Eastern fashion about a court, with only blank outside walls, was no place in which to pass a long invalidism, and three days later my father had me carried to the steamer, and, crossing to Gibraltar, we traveled by easy railroad trips to Leipzig. We had left our belongings with Jastrow, and he begged us, on our arrival, to become members of his household, which we were only too glad to do for a time. His joy over my return was most touching, and he and Humzel both seemed to regard me very much as if I were the creation of their own brains, who was to bring them immortal fame in time. My father had long before counseled me to be a pursuer of knowledge, and not of money; telling me the winning of the latter narrowed the intellect and stunted the finer qualities of one's nature, making all men natural enemies, while the acquisition of the former broadened one's mind, developed the nobility within, and engendered love of one's associates. These two men illustrated his theory, and had my tendency been avaricious I think their unselfish love and example would have made me otherwise. And yet, how dare I claim to be free from sordidness, when all my thoughts and hopes and daily life are now bent on winning money?

My leg was far too troublesome to permit me to sit at a desk, but my father insisted on being my scribe; and thus, lying on a lounge, I began part of the work I had so long planned, taking up for my first book the Turkish irruption, the crusades against the Saracens, and their subsequent history. Thinking so much of you, both as the child who had won my boyish heart and as the beautiful woman whose face had fascinated and moved me so deeply, I do not know how, except for my work, I should have lived through those long and weary months of enforced inaction while my leg so slowly knit.

More as recreation from this serious endeavor than as supplementary labor, I gathered the articles I had written for the Deutsche Rundshau and the Revue des Deux Mondes from time to time in our travels, and with new material from my journal I worked the whole into a popular account of what we had seen and done. While I still used a walking-stick I was reading proof of the German edition, and my English replica, rather than translation, was under negotiation through my publisher for London and New York editions. My father, who busied himself with a French version, insisted that the book would be a great success, and the articles under my assumed name had been so well noticed that I was myself hopeful of what better work in book form might do for my reputation; for against his advice, I had determined to abandon my pseudonym.

But all these schemes and hopes were forgotten in the illness of my father. Contrary to my wishes, he had overworked himself in the French translation, while his life, for months of my enforced inactivity, had been one long service, impossible for me to avoid or refuse without giving him pain. This double exertion proved too great a strain. The day after he sent the manuscript to Paris, as he sat conning the sheets of the concluding chapter of my history, he laid them down without a word, and, leaning forward, quietly rested his head upon the table. I was by his side and had him on the sofa in an instant, where he lay unconscious till the doctor came. We were told that it was a slight stroke, and by the next day he seemed quite well. But slowly he lost the use of one side, and within a week was helpless. I like to remember that I was well enough to tend him as he had tended me. He lingered for a month, sweet and gentle as always; then, one evening, as I sat beside him, he opened his eyes and said, "Good-night, Don. Good-night, Maizie." And with those words his loving soul went back to its Creator.

I found about his neck a ribbon to which was attached a locket containing the long tress you cut off for him that day in the Bois, one of my mother's curls, and a little tow-colored lock which I suppose was my own hair before it darkened,—a locket I have since worn unchanged, because, sadly discordant though such association has become, I cannot bring myself to separate what he tied together. It seems to symbolize his love for all of us.

The kindness of my friends I can never forget. I was so broken down as really to be unfit for thought, and their generous foresight did everything possible to spare me trouble or pain. Especially to Professor and Frau Jastrow do I owe an unpayable debt, for they made me feel that there was still some one in whose love I stood first; and had I been the child who had never come to them, I question if they could have done more for me than they did.

One thing that I had to do myself was to notify my mother of my father's death. From the time she had quitted us my father and I had avoided mention of her; but during his illness he asked me to write in case of his death, and gave me her New York address, from which I inferred that in some way he had kept himself informed concerning her, though I feel very certain that she had never written him. That I had never tried to learn anything myself was due to the estrangement, but still more to my interest in my studies and work. Now I wrote her, as I had promised, telling her briefly the circumstances of my father's illness and death, and offering to write fuller details if she wished to know them. I would not feign love for her, but I wrote tenderly of him and without coldness to her. She never replied.

Kind as were all my intimates, I craved more than friendship, however loving it might be. One of the two great loves of my life had gone out from it, and, in the gap it left, the other became doubly dear to me. The wish to see you grew and strengthened each day, until at last it shaped my plans, and I announced my intention to visit America; making the specious explanation that, after my long invalidism and grief, the change would be the best specific for me.

At this time I received the offer of appointment as professor extraordinarius of philology and ethnology under Jastrow, another manifestation of his love; but till I had seen you I would not bind myself by accepting, and through his influence I was given three months to consider my answer. I seem doomed never to requite the services of those I love the most, but I am glad that in the nine months which I passed under his roof my knowledge of the Eastern dialects had pushed his work so much nearer completion.

Leaving all my possessions behind except the manuscript of my history, I started on my voyage of love. For two days I tarried in Paris, settling my little property. I had long known that the flotsam of my father's fortune, wrecked in Wall Street, was a few bonds deposited with Paris bankers; and when I called upon the firm it was merely to continue the old arrangement, by which they cut the coupons and placed them to my bank credit. It was in this visit that I searched out our old pension, and sat dreaming in the park. How could I imagine, remembering those days of closest love and sympathy, and knowing too your kindness to one you thought a mere Eastern stroller, that you could have changed so to your former friend?

The most curious fact to me, in looking back upon that time, is that the idea never occurred to me that you were a married woman. It never entered my thoughts that a beauty which fascinated and drew me so far from my natural orbit must be an equally powerful charm to other men. As for Mr. Blodgett, I never gave him a second thought, not even accounting for his relations with you. My foolishness, I suppose, is typical of the scholar's abstraction and impracticality.

As the steamer neared New York, my impatience to see you increased apace. Far from longing for our old ten-day passage, I found a voyage of seven days too long. Ridiculous as it may seem, I almost lost my temper at the slowness of the customs examination. I believe I was half mad, and only marvel that I did so sane a thing as to go to a hotel, change my clothes, and dine, before attempting to see you.

I ascertained Mr. Walton's address the moment I reached my hotel, and sent a messenger there to inquire your whereabouts. He brought me back word that Mr. Walton was absent from the city, but the servant had informed him that you still lived with your uncle and that you were in town.

I cannot tell you the surprise and joy I felt when, on arriving at your house on Madison Avenue that evening, I discovered it to be our old habitat. It seemed as if your selection of that as your home, probably from sentiment, was a bow of promise for the future, and I rang the bell, almost trembling with emotion and happiness.

The footman showed me to the drawing-room and took my card. All inside, so far as I could see, was changed past the point of recognition, but everything was beautiful, and I felt in that one room that no decorator's conventional taste had formed its harmony, but that an artistic sense had planned the whole. What a contrast it was to the old days of untasteful and untidy richness!

I sat but a moment before the footman returned. Looking not at me, but over my head, and with an attitude and air as deferential as if I were the guest of all others most welcome, he said, "Miss Walton declines the honor of Mr. Maitland's acquaintance, and begs to be excused."

The blow came so suddenly, and was so crushing, that for a moment I lost my dignity. "There must be some mistake!" I exclaimed. "You gave Miss Walton my card?"

The footman only bowed assent.

"Go to Miss Walton and say I must see her a moment."

"Miss Walton instructed me to add, in case Mr. Maitland persisted, that she prefers to hold no intercourse with Mr. Maitland and will receive no messages from him."

Pride came to my rescue, and I passed silently into the hall. The servant opened the door, and I went out from my old home, never to enter it more. At the foot of the steps I turned and looked back, hardly yet believing what I had been told. Even in the sting and humiliation of that moment my love was stronger than the newer sensations. I said, "Good-night, Maizie. God keep you," and walked away.

VIII

February 27. I sat for hours in my room, that night, trying to find some solution of the mystery and groping for a future course of action. I thought of a visit to my mother, on the chance that she would give me the key to the puzzle, but could not bring myself to it. Rejecting that idea, I decided to seek out Mr. Blodgett, who, being your friend, might know the reason for what you had done.

Finding on inquiry, the next morning, that Mr. Blodgett was a member of one of the chief banking firms of New York, I went to his office. The ante-room was well filled with people anxious to see the great banker, and the door-boy refused me access to him without giving my name and business. Knowing that "Donald Maitland" would mean nothing to Mr. Blodgett, and might even fail to secure me an audience, I wrote on a slip of paper, "A seeker of knowledge from the Altai Mountains." Nor was I wrong, for the boy, on his return, gave me immediate entrance, and another moment brought me face to face with my once-disliked countryman.

His hand was extended to greet me, but as he looked at my face his arm dropped in surprise. "Your name, please?" he demanded, with a business-like clip to his voice, at the same time picking up and glancing quickly at three or four cards and slips of paper that were on the corner of his desk.

"I am the attorney for ancient peoples," I announced, smiling, "come to thank the New World for its kindness to a broken-legged man."

Instantly Mr. Blodgett smiled too, and again extended his hand. "Glad to see you," he said. "Sit down." Then looking at me keenly, he added, "You've done a lot of bleaching or scrubbing since we met."

"In the interval my face has been hidden from the sun-god of my fathers."

"Ah!" Then his Americanism cropped out by a question: "Are you European or Asiatic?—for you are too dark to be the one, and too white to be the other."

"My parents were American, and I was born in New York."

"The deuce you were! Then why were you masquerading in Arab dress and with a brown face in Tangier, and why did you say you came from some mountains in Asia?"

"I was for the time an Arab, and I was last from the Altai Mountains," I explained, and smilingly added, "Is my explanation satisfactory?"

"Well, I suppose you spoke by the book," he replied. "Wherever you were born, I'm glad to see—Hold on!" he cried, interrupting his own speech. "Why did you call yourself Dr. Rudolph Hartzmann, of Leipzig, if you were an American?"

"I did not," I denied, startled by his question, for my identity with the pseudonym was known only to my professors and publishers.

"You weren't living in Tangier under the name of Hartzmann?" he inquired.

"No."

"Then how came it that when my servant was sent to leave some fruit and flowers for you and inquire your name, he was told that you were Dr. Rudolph Hartzmann, of Leipzig?"

"Are you serious?" I questioned, as much puzzled as he for the moment.

"Never more so. I remember our astonishment to think that any European should have so dark a skin and live in the native quarter."

"Mr. Blodgett," I explained, "I did not know till this moment that a pen name I have used to sign my writings had been given you, but it was a joke of my father's to register me under it, and my only theory is that he had given some one in the hotel that name, and, by mischance, your servant was misinformed."

He was too good a business man to look as skeptical as he probably felt, and merely asked, "What is your real name, then?"

"Donald Maitland, son of William Maitland."

His eyes gave a startled wink and he screwed his lips into position for a whistle, but checking the inclination, he merely turned his revolving-chair so that he looked out of a window. He sat thus for a moment, and then, facing me, he questioned, with a sudden curtness of voice and manner, "What is your business with me?"

"I have taken the liberty of calling on the supposition that you are a friend of Miss Walton."

"I am."

"Miss Walton was once my father's ward, yet last night she refused to see me. Can you tell me why?"

"The reason is rather obvious," he asserted crisply.

"Will you tell me what it is?"

He looked at me from under his gray eyebrows. "Is that all you want of me?" he demanded.

"Yes."

"Well, then, Miss Walton refused to see you because she despises you."

I felt my cheeks burn, but I gripped the arm of my chair and waited till I could speak coolly; then I asked, "For what?"

"You are ignorant of the fact that your father embezzled a part of Miss Walton's fortune, and that you and he have since lived upon it?" he exclaimed, with no veiling of his contempt.

I sat calmly, for the idea was too new, and I had too many connecting links to recall, to have the full horror of the disgrace come home to me at once. He did not give me time for thought, but interrogated, "Well?"

Having to speak, I asked, "You are sure of what you say?"

"Sure!" he ejaculated. "Why, it's been known to every one for years, and I was one of the trustees appointed by the court to look out for Miss Walton's interest in what property your father couldn't take with him!"

"If you are a trustee of Miss Walton," I said, growing cool in my agony of shame, "can you spare me five minutes and answer some questions?"

That I did not deny knowledge of the wrong seemed to raise me in his opinion, for he nodded his head and looked less stern.

"How much did my father—How much did Miss Walton lose?" I inquired.

"One hundred and thirty thousand was all the property he could negotiate, and we succeeded, by bidding in his house over the mortgage and by taking the library at a valuation, in recovering twenty-six thousand."

"Was that amount net?"

"Yes."

"Then in 1879 the amount due Miss Walton was one hundred and four thousand dollars?"

"Yes."

"Thank you, Mr. Blodgett," I added, rising. "I am only sorry, after your former kindness, to have given you this further trouble. I am grateful for both." In my shame I did not dare to offer him my hand, but he held out his.

"Mr. Maitland," he rejoined, "I'm a pretty good judge of men, and I don't believe you have done wrong knowingly."

"I never dreamed it," I almost sobbed, shaking his hand.

"It's pretty rough," he said. "I hope you won't show the white feather by doing anything desperate?"

I shook my head, and walked to the door. As I reached it a new thought occurred to me, and, turning, I asked, "What has the legal rate of interest been since 1879?"

For reply he touched an electric button on his desk, and I heard the lock click in the door by which I stood. He pulled a chair near his own, and commanded, "Come here and sit down," in such a peremptory tone that I obeyed. "Why did you ask that question?" he catechised.

"That I may find out how much I owe Miss Walton."

"What for?"

"To attempt restitution."

"I hope you know what you're talking about?"

"I'm still rather confused, but so much I can see clearly enough."

"How much property have you?"

"My father left me something over thirty-one thousand dollars."

"Thirty-one from one hundred and four leaves seventy-three."

"And interest," I corrected.

"I thought that was what you were driving at," he surmised calmly. He pulled out a volume from its repository in his desk, and turned backwards and forwards in the book for a few moments, taking off figures on a sheet of paper. "Eight years at five per cent makes the whole over one hundred and fifty-five thousand dollars less thirty-one."

"Thank you."

"Where can you get the balance?"

"I must earn it."

He looked at me with a slightly quizzical expression and asked, "How?"

"That I have yet to think out."

"Any business?"

"I have the offer of a professorship at Leipzig, but that's out of the question now."

"Why?"

"It would give me only two thousand a year at first, and the interest on the debt will be over six thousand annually."

"What do you know?" he questioned.

"Most of the languages and dialects of Europe and Asia, and a good deal of history and ethnology. I am fairly read in arts, sciences, and religions, and I know something of writing," I answered, smiling at the absurdity of mentioning such knowledge in the face of such a condition.

"Humph! And you'd have sold all that for two thousand a year?"

"I think so."

"Well, that only proves that a man had better cultivate his gumption, and not his brains!"

"If he wishes to make money," I could not help retorting gently.

"You're just like Maizie!" he sniffed, and his going back to your familiar name in my presence was the best compliment he could have paid me. "You two ought to have died young and gone to heaven, where there's nothing to do but cultivate the soul."

"I wish we had!"

"Why don't you go to your mother?"

"For what?"

"For the money."

"Has she money?"

"Yes. She had a little money when she married your father, which she kept tight hold of; her mother's death, two years ago, gave her more, and she has just married a rich man."

"I don't know yet what I shall do," I replied, rising.

"Well," he advised kindly, "before you blow your brains out or do anything else that's a waste of good material, come and see me again."

"Thank you," I responded. "And, Mr. Blodgett, as a favor, I ask that all I have told you, and even my presence in New York, shall be confidential between us."

"Nonsense!" he growled. "I shall tell Maizie all about it."

"Miss Walton least of any," I begged.

"Why don't you insist, too, that Mrs. Blodgett, who intends that I shall inform her nightly of everything I know, sha'n't be told?" he queried.

"It grieves me to be a marplot of connubial confidences," I rejoined, responding to his smile, "but this must be between us."

"Have your own way," he acceded, and then laughed. "I'll have a good time over it, for I'll let Mrs. Blodgett see there is a secret, and she'll go crazy trying to worm it out of me."

He shook my hand again, and I felt ashamed to think that his voice and manner had once made me hold him in contempt.

I went back to the hotel, and thought over the past, seeing how blind I had been. Now for the first time everything became clear. I understood the trip to Europe and our remaining there, why my mother had left us, why Mr. Walton had been permitted to take you from us without protest, why we had not mingled with Americans, and my father's motives in making me write under a pen name, in registering me at hotels by it, and in giving that name to your servant. Now it was obvious why he never signed his articles, and why he appealed to me to let him aid me to make a reputation: it was his endeavor to atone to me for the wrong he had done.

Good-night, my love.

IX

February 28. Many times in the last three years I have begun a letter to you, for the thought that you, like the rest of the world, may rank my father with other embezzlers stings me almost to desperation. Each time it has been to tear the attempted justification—or I should say, extenuation—into fragments, long before it was completed. In all my trials I have come to realize that nothing I can say can stand him in stead; for whatever I urge is open to suspicion, not merely because it is my interest to condone his act, but still more because it inevitably becomes an indirect justification of myself, and therefore, in a sense, a plea for pardon.

At moments, too, when with you, I have had to exercise the greatest self-control not to tell you what I feel. If I were only some one else than Donald Maitland, so that I might say to you:—

"You should know that your guardian was incapable of the lowness the world imputes to him! I am not trying to belittle the sin, but to distinguish the motive. His wrong was no mean attempt to enrich himself at the expense of one he loved, for his nature was wholly unmercenary, and his transgression originated, not through greed, but through lack of it. Like all men of true intellect, he was heedless in money matters, and I am conscious that there was in him, as there is in me, the certain weakness which is almost inevitable with mind cultivation,—an engulfing, as it were, of the big principles of right and wrong in the complexities and the refinements of cultivated thought. His birthright was scholarship, but in place of the life he was fitted for he was forced into Wall Street, and toiled there without sympathy or aptitude for his work. Do you not remember how, aside from our companionship, his books were his one great pleasure? The wealth of mind he gave to us tells the story of how he must have neglected his office in favor of his library. Yet though this preference might have made him a poor man, I cannot think his studies would ever have led him into dishonesty. I have never had the heart to trace the history of his act, but Mr. Blodgett tells me that shortly after his marriage he first began to speculate, and knowing as I do my mother's extravagance and my father's love for her, I can understand the motive. The inevitable result came presently, and, as a temporary expedient, a small part of your property was used. Then a desperate attempt was made to recover this by the risking of a larger portion, and after that there was nothing left but confession or flight. I wish he had spoken, but the weakness that produced the first wrong accounts for the second, and I believe his chief thought was of me, and how I might be saved from the consequences of his guilt. Unless you have put him wholly out of your heart, you must appreciate that it was no sordid scheme to cheat you, but a surrender to the love strong enough to overcome his honesty. You must know that he loved you too well to wrong you willingly, and I think with pain of what I am sure he must have suffered in his shame at having robbed you. Do you not remember the sadness in his face in those later years, and his tenderness to both of us? Can you not see that his kindness, his patience, and his care of us were his endeavored atonement?"

Oh, Maizie, I ask nothing for myself, but if you could be brought to think of him, to love him, as you once did, my greatest grief would be ended.

Bitter as my misery was after Mr. Blodgett's revelation, there was still some sweetness to make it bearable. For years I had thought of you as heartless and forgetful, and even in my love had hated and despised you at moments, as only love can hate and despise. The world thinks that animosity is always strongest against enemies, though daily it sees the intensest feuds between those nations and individuals who are most closely related, and never learns that the deepest hatred comes from love. Now I knew that you had cause for slighting my letters and gift, and the knowledge of my injustice and the thought that you were more lovable than ever were the silver lining to my cloud of shame.

My first meeting with you was a pure chance, yet it shaped my life. For three weeks after my call on Mr. Blodgett I pondered and vacillated over what I should do, without reaching any decision. At the end of that time I went to his office again.

"Mr. Blodgett has asked two or three times if you hadn't called," the boy informed me; adding, as he opened the door to the private office, "He told me, if you ever came again, sir, to show you right in."

I passed through the doorway, and then faltered, for you were sitting beside the banker, overlooking a paper that he was commenting upon. Could I have escaped unnoticed, I should have done so; but you both glanced up as I entered.

The moment you saw me you rose, with an exclamation of recognition and surprise, which meant to me that you knew your old friend in spite of the changes. Do you wonder that, not foreseeing what was to come, I stood there as if turned to stone? My manner evidently made you question your own eyes, for you asked, "Is not this Dr. Hartzmann?"

"Of course it is!" cried Mr. Blodgett, with a quickness and heartiness which proved that your question was almost as great a relief to him as it was to me.

"I did not think, Miss Walton," I replied, steadying my voice as best I could, "that you saw my face clearly enough that evening, to recollect it?"

"The moonlight was so strong," you explained, "that I should have known you anywhere."

"Then your eyes are better than mine," asserted Mr. Blodgett. "I accused the doctor of using blondine, to atone for my not recognizing him, though I must confess he will have to use a good deal more if he wants to be thought anything but Italian."

"Then you have met before?" you questioned.

"Yes," replied Mr. Blodgett. "I was going to tell you when we got through with that mortgage. I knew you would be interested to hear that the doctor was in New York. Seems like Tangier, doesn't it?"

"In reminiscence," I assented, merely to gain time.

"None of your rickety ruins," chuckled Mr. Blodgett.

"But more ruin," you said.

"And more danger," I added, pointing out of the window at the passers-by in Wall Street. "Nowhere in my travels, even among races that have to go armed, have I ever seen so many anxious and careworn faces."

"Most of them look worried," suggested Mr. Blodgett, "only because they are afraid they'll take more than three minutes to eat their lunch."

For a moment you spoke with Mr. Blodgett on business, and then offered me your hand in farewell, saying, "I am very glad, Dr. Hartzmann, for this chance reunion. Mr. Blodgett and I have often spoken of the mysterious Oriental who fell in—and out—of our knowledge so strangely."

"I have wished to meet you, Miss Walton," I responded warmly, "to thank you for your kindness and help to me when"—

"That was nothing, Dr. Hartzmann," you interrupted, in evident deprecation of my thanks. "Indeed, I have always felt that we were in a measure responsible for your accident, and that we made but a poor return by the little we did. Good-morning."

Mr. Blodgett took you to your carriage, and when he returned he gave a whistle. "Well!" he exclaimed. "I haven't gone through such a ten-second scare since I proposed to my superior moiety."

"I ought"—I began.

But he went on: "There's nothing frightens me so much as a wrought-up woman. Dynamite or volcanoes aren't a circumstance to her, because they have limits; but woman!"

I laughed and said, "The Hindoos have a paradox to the effect that women fear mice, mice fear men, and men fear women."

"She got so much better and longer look at you in Tangier than I did that I don't wonder she recognized Dr. Hartzmann when I didn't. But why did she stop there in her recollections?"

"It appeared incomprehensible to me for a moment, yet, as a fact, her knowing me as Donald Maitland would have been the greater marvel of the two. When she knew me, I was an undersized, pallid, stooping lad of seventeen. In the ten years since, my hair and skin have both darkened greatly, I have grown a mustache, and my voice has undergone the change that comes with manhood, as well as that which comes by speaking foreign tongues. Your very question as to whether I was of Eastern birth tells the whole story, for such a doubt would seem absurd to one who remembered the boy of ten years ago. Then, too, Miss Walton, having recognized me as Dr. Hartzmann, was, as it were, disarmed of all suspicion by having no question-mark in her mind as to my exact identity."

Mr. Blodgett nodded his head in assent. "And you don't know it all," he informed me. "I'm going to be frank, doctor, and acknowledge that I've expressed a pretty low opinion of you to her more than once. If Maizie were asked what man in this world she'd be least likely to meet in my office on a friendly footing, she would probably think of you. Your presence here was equivalent to saying that you weren't Donald Maitland, let alone the fact that I greeted you as Dr. Hartzmann, and that she could never dream of my having a reason to deceive her in your identity."

"Such a chain of circumstances almost makes one believe in kismet," I sighed. Then I laughed, and added, "How easy it is to show that one need not be scared—after the danger is all over!"

"That isn't the only scare I owe to you," muttered Mr. Blodgett. "I didn't take your address because I told you to come again. Why didn't you?"

"I am here."

"Yes. But for three weeks I've been worrying over what you were doing with yourself, and not knowing that you hadn't cut your throat."

"I am sorry to have troubled you. I stayed away to save troubling you."

"You're as considerate as the Fiji islander was of the missionary, when he asked him if he had rather be cooked *à la maître d'hôtel* or *en papillote*. What have you been doing?"

"Very little to any purpose. I have written to my publisher, offering to sell my rights in my text-books; to a friend, asking him to learn for what price he can sell my library; and to my bankers, directing them to send me the bonds and a draft for my balance. I received the securities and a bill of exchange yesterday, and am so ignorant of business methods that I came to you this morning to learn how to turn them into cash."

"I'll do better than that," volunteered Mr. Blodgett, touching a button. "Give them to me, and I'll have it done." Then, after he had turned the matter over to a clerk, he asked, "What does your publisher offer?"

"Thirty-five hundred."

"And what are your royalties?"

"Last year they were over six hundred dollars."

"Humph! That's equivalent to investing money at eighteen per cent. You ought to get more than that."

"A little more or less is nothing compared with paying so much on my debt."

"What will your library bring?"

"Perhaps four thousand, if I can find some one who wants so technical a collection."

"And you can get along without it?"

"I must," I declared, though wincing a little.

"Rather goes against the grain, eh?" he rejoined kindly.

I tried to laugh, and said, "My books have been such good comrades that I haven't quite accustomed myself yet to thinking of them as merchandise. I feel a little as the bankrupt planter must have felt when he saw his slave children offered for sale."

"And what do you plan to do with yourself?"

"I haven't been able to make up my mind."

We were interrupted at this point by some business matter, and I took my leave. The next morning Mr. Blodgett called at my boarding-place on his way down town.

"I haven't come to talk business," he announced. "I told my wife and daughter, last night, about the fellow from the backwoods of Asia, and made them so curious that Mrs. Blodgett has given me permission to furnish him board and lodgings for a week. I'll promise you a better room than this," he added, glancing at the box I had moved into as soon as I realized how much worse than a pauper I was.

I could hardly express my gratitude as I tried to thank him, but he pretended not to perceive my emotion, and said briskly: "That's settled, then. Send your stuff round any time to-day, and be on deck for a seven-o'clock dinner."

You, who know Mrs. Blodgett so much better than I, can understand my bewilderment during the first day or two of my visit. Her husband had jokingly pictured me as of an Eastern race, which made the meeting rather embarrassing; but the moment she comprehended that I did not habitually sit on the floor, did not carry a scimiter or kris, and was not unwashed and ferine, but only a dark skinned, dark haired, and very silent German scholar, she took possession of me as I have seen her do of others. She preceded me to my room, ringing for a servant on the way, made me open my trunk, and directed the maid where to put each article it contained. She told me what time to be ready for dinner, what to wear for it, and at that meal she had me helped twice to such dishes as she chose, while refusing to let me have more than one cup of coffee. To a man who had never had any one to look after him in small things it was a novel and rather pleasant if surprising experience, and when I grew accustomed to it I easily understood Mr. Blodgett's chuckles of enjoyment when she told him he shouldn't have a third cigar, when she decided how close he was to sit to the fire, and finally when she made all of us—Agnes, Mr. Blodgett, and myself—go to bed at her own hour for retiring. Best of all I understood Mr. Blodgett's familiar name for her, "the boss." That visit was a perfect revelation to me of affectionate, thoughtful, and persistently minute domineering. I do not believe that the man lives, though he be the veriest woman-hater, who could help loving her after a fortnight of her tyranny. Certainly I could not.

By Mr. Blodgett's aid I secured a "paper" cable transfer of the money realized from the bonds and draft, in order that it might seem to come from Europe, and sent it to you, writing at his suggestion, "The inclosed draft on Foster G. Blodgett & Co. for the sum of thirty-three thousand dollars is part payment of principal and interest due you from estate of William G. Maitland." I wonder what your thoughts were as you read the unsigned and typewritten note?

It was your greeting of me by my alias that led me to accept the incognito. Perhaps it was cowardly to shirk my shame by such a means, but it was not done from cowardice; the thought did not even occur to me until it opened a way to knowing you. And in that hope my very misery became almost happiness, for its possibilities seemed those of the Oriental poet who wrote:—

> "My love once offered me a bitter draught
> From which in cowardice I flinched.
> But still she tendered to me;
> And bowing to her wish, I then no longer shrank,
> But took the cup and put it to my lips.
> Oh, marvel! gazing still at her,
> The potion turned to sweetness as I drank."

If your old friend, Donald Maitland, were dead to you, your new lover, Rudolph Hartzmann, might fill his place. I never stopped to think if such trickery were right, or rather my love was stronger than my conscience.

Good-night, my dearest.

X

March 1. During my visit I heard much about you from Mrs. Blodgett and Agnes, for your name was constantly on their lips. From them I learned that your birth, wealth, and the influence of your uncle had involved you in a fashionable society for which you cared nothing, and that, aside from the gayety which that circle forced upon you, your time was spent in travel, and in reading, music, and charitable work. Except for themselves, they averred, you had no intimate friends, and their explanation of this fact proved to me that you had taken our separation as seriously as had I.

"After Mr. Walton brought her to America she spent the first few months with us," Mrs. Blodgett told me, "and was the loneliest child I ever saw. Her big eyes used to look so wistfully at times that I could hardly bear it, yet not a word did she ever speak of her sorrow. And all on account of that wretch and his son! I think the worse men are, the more a good woman loves them! When Maizie was old enough to understand, and Mr. Walton told her how she had been robbed, she wouldn't believe him till Mr. Blodgett confirmed the story. She used to be always talking of the two, but she has never spoken of them since that night."

Even more cruel to me was something Agnes related. She worshiped you with the love and admiration a girl of eighteen sometimes feels for a girl of twenty-three, and in singing your praises,—to a most willing listener,—one day, she exclaimed, "Oh, I wish I were a man, so that I could be her lover! I'd make her believe in love." Then seeing my questioning look, Agnes continued: "What with her selfish old uncle, and the men who want to marry her for her money, and those hateful Maitlands, she has been made to distrust all love and friendship. She has the idea that she isn't lovable,— that people don't like her for herself; and I really think she will never marry, just because of it."

Better far than this knowledge of you at second-hand was Mr. Blodgett's telling me that you were to dine with them during my visit. It may seem absurd, but not the least part of my eagerness that night was to see you in evening dress. If I had not loved you already, I should have done so from that meeting; and although you are dear to me for many things besides your beauty, I understand why men love you so deeply who know nothing of your nature. That all men should not love you is my only marvel whenever I recall that first glimpse of you as you entered the Blodgetts' drawing-room.

Before we had finished our greetings Mr. Whitely entered, and though I little realized how vital a part he was to be of my life, I yet regarded him with instant interest, for something in his manner towards you suggested to me that he coveted the hand you offered him.

A lover does not view a rival kindly, but I am compelled to own that he is handsome. If I had the right to cavil, I could criticise only his mouth, which it seems to me has slyness with a certain cruel firmness; but I did not notice this until I knew him better, and perhaps it is only my imagination, born of later knowledge. I am not so blinded by my jealousy as to deny his perfect manner, for one feels the polished surface, touch the outside where one will.

Your demeanor towards him was friendly, yet with all its graciousness it seemed to me to have a quality not so much of aloofness as of limit; conveying in an indefinable way the fact that such relations as then existed between you were the only possible ones. It was a shading so imperceptible that I do not think the Blodgetts realized it, and I should have questioned if Mr. Whitely himself were conscious of it, but for one or two things he said in the course of the evening, which had to me, under the veil of a general topic, individual suggestion.

We were discussing that well-worn question of woman's education, Mrs. Blodgett having introduced the apple of discord by a sweeping disapproval of college education for women, on the ground that it prevented their marrying.

"They get to know too much, eh?" laughed Mr. Blodgett.

"No," cried Mrs. Blodgett, "they get to know too little! While they ought to be out in the world studying life and men, so as to choose wisely, they're shut up in dormitories filling their brains with Greek and mathematics."

"You would limit a woman's arithmetic to the solution of how to make one and one, one?" I asked, smiling.

"Surely, Mrs. Blodgett, you do not mean that an uncultivated woman makes the best wife?" inquired Mr. Whitely.

"I mean," rejoined Mrs. Blodgett, "that women who know much of books know little of men. That's why over-intellectual women always marry fools."

"How many intellectual wives there must be!" you said.

"I shouldn't mind if they only married fools," continued Mrs. Blodgett, "but half the time they don't marry at all."

"Does that prove or disprove their intellect?" you asked.

"It means," replied Mrs. Blodgett, "that they are so puffed up with their imaginary knowledge that they think no man good enough for them."

"I've known one or two college boys graduate with the same large ideas," remarked Mr. Blodgett.

"But a man gets over it after a few years," urged Mrs. Blodgett, "and is none the worse off; but by the time a girl overcomes the idea, she's so old that no man worth having will look at her."

"I rather think, Mrs. Blodgett," said Mr. Whitely, in that charmingly deferential manner he has with women, "that some men do not try to win highly educated women because they are abashed by a sense of their own inferiority."

"Where do those men hide themselves, Whitely?" interrogated Mr. Blodgett.

"I'll not question the reason," retorted Mrs. Blodgett. "The fact that over-educated girls think themselves above men is all I claim."

"I don't think, Mrs. Blodgett," you corrected, "it is so much a feeling of superiority as it is a change in the aims of marriage. Formerly, woman married to gain a protector, and man to gain a housewife. Now, matrimony is sought far less for service, and far more for companionship."

"But, Miss Walton," questioned Mr. Whitely, "does not the woman ask too much nowadays? She has the leisure to read and study, but a business man cannot spare the time. Is it fair, then, to expect that he shall be as cultivated as she can make herself?"

"That is, I think, the real cause for complaint," you answered. "The business man is so absorbed in money-making that he sacrifices his whole time to it. I can understand a woman falling in love with a lance or a sword, dull companions though they must have been, but it seems to me impossible for any woman to love a minting-machine, even though she might be driven to marry it for its product."

"That's rough on us, Whitely," laughed Mr. Blodgett good-naturedly; but Mr. Whitely reddened, and you, as if to divert the subject from this personal tendency, turned and surmised to me:—

"I suppose that as a German, Dr. Hartzmann, you think a woman should be nothing more than a housekeeper?"

"Why not suggest, Miss Walton," I replied, smiling, "that as an Orientalist I must think the seraglio woman's proper sphere?"

"But, Miss Walton," persisted Mr. Whitely, not accepting your diversion, "a man, to be successful nowadays, must give all his attention to his business.

"I presume that is so," you acceded; "but could he not be content with a little less success in money-making, and strive to acquire a few more amenities?"

"Maizie wants us all to be painters and poets and musicians," asserted Mr. Blodgett.

"Not at all," you denied.

"Oh, Maizie!" cried Agnes. "You know you said the other day that you hoped I wouldn't marry a business man."

"I said '*only* a business man,' Agnes," you replied, without a trace of the embarrassment so many women would have shown. "Because men cannot all be clergymen is no reason for their knowing nothing of religion. There would be no painters, poets, or musicians if there were no dilettanti."

"Yet I think," argued Mr. Whitely, still as if he were trying to convince you of something, "that the successful business man has as much brain as most writers or artists."

"I have no doubt that is true," you assented. "So, too, a day laborer may have a good mind. But of what avail is a brain if it has never been trained, or has been trained to know only one thing?"

"But authors and painters are only specialists," urged Mr. Whitely.

"They are specialists of a very different type," you responded, "from the man whose daily thoughts are engrossed with the prices of pig-iron or cotton sheetings. I think one reason why American girls frequently marry Europeans is that the foreign man is so apt to be more broadly cultivated."

"That's what I mean by saying that books unfit women to marry wisely," interjected Mrs. Blodgett. "They marry foreigners because they are more cultivated, without a thought of character."

"Indeed, Mrs. Blodgett," you observed, "has not the day gone by for thinking dullness a sign of honesty? And certainly a business career is far more likely to corrupt and harden men's natures than the higher professions, for its temptations and strifes are so much greater."

Your opinion was so in accord with what my father had often preached that I could not but wonder if his teachings still colored your thoughts. To test this idea as well as to learn your present view, I recurred to another theory of his by saying, "Does not the broader and more sensitive nature of the scholar or artist involve defects fully as serious as the hardness and narrowness of the business man? Some one has said that 'to marry a literary man is to domesticate a bundle of nerves.'"

"A nervous irritability," you replied, "which came from fine mental exertion, would be as nothing compared to my own fretting over enforced companionship with an unsympathetic or sordid nature." Then you laughed, and added, "I must have a very bad temper, for it is the only one which ever really annoys me."

That last speech told me how thoroughly the woman of twenty-three was a development of the child of fourteen, for I remembered how little my mother's anger used to disturb you, but how deeply and strongly your emotions affected you. I suppose it was absurd, but I felt happy to think that you had changed so little in character from the time when I knew you so well. And from that evening I never for an instant believed that you would marry Mr. Whitely, for I was sure that you could never love him. How could I dream that you, with beauty, social position, and wealth, would make a loveless marriage?

Good-night, my love.

XI

March 2. The truth of the difference of quality between the business man and the scholar was quickly brought home to me. On the last evening of my visit, Mr. Blodgett revealed the reason for his latest kindness. "I got you here," he explained, "to look you over and see what you were fit for, thinking I might work you in somewhere. No," he continued, as he saw the questioning hopefulness on my face, "you wouldn't do in business. You've got a sight too much conscience and sympathy, and a sight too little drive. All business is getting the best of somebody else, and you're the kind of chap who'd let a fellow up just because you'd got him down." Seeing the sadness in my face, for I knew too well he had fathomed me, he added kindly, "Don't get chicken-hearted over what I say. It's easy enough to outwit a man; the hard thing is not to do it. I'd go out of the trade to-morrow, if it weren't for the boss and Agnes, for I get tired of the meanness of the whole thing. But they want to cut a figure, and that isn't to be done in this town for nothing. I'll find something for you yet that sha'n't make you sell your heart and your soul as well as your time."

I was too full of my love and my purpose, however, for this to discourage me. The moment my determination to remain in New York was taken, I wrote to Jastrow, Humzel, and others of my German friends, telling them that for business reasons I had decided to be known as Rudolph Hartzmann, and asking if they would stretch friendship so far as to give me letters in that name to such American publishers and editors as they knew. Excepting Jastrow, they all responded with introductions so flattering that I was almost ashamed to present them, and he wrote me that he had not offered my books for sale, and begged me to reconsider my refusal of the professorship. He even offered, if I would accept the appointment, to divide with me his tuition fees, and suggested that his own advancing years were a pledge that his position would erelong be vacant for me to step into. It almost broke my heart to have to write him that I could not accept his generous offer. In July I received a second letter from him, most touching in its attempt to keep back the grief he felt, but yielding to my determination. He sent me many good introductions, and submitted a bid for my library from a bookseller; but knowing the books to be worth at least double the offer, I held the sale in abeyance.

My first six months in New York disheartened me greatly, though now I know that I succeeded far better than I could have expected to do, in the dullness of the summer. My work was the proof-reading of my book of travel in its varying polyglots, seeing through the press English versions of my two text-books, and writing a third in both English and German. Furthermore, my letters of introduction had made me known to a number of the professors of Columbia College, and by their influence I received an appointment to deliver a course of lectures on race movements the following winter; so I prepared my notes in this leisure time. But this work was far too little to fill my time, and I wrote all kinds of editorials, essays, and reviews, fairly wearing out the editors of the various magazines and newspapers with my frequent calls and articles. Finally I attempted to sell my books to several libraries; but though the tomes and the price both tempted several, none had the money to spend on such a collection.

My book of travel was published in September, was praised by the reviews, and at once sprang into a good sale for a work of that class; for Europe is interested in whatever bears on her cancer growth, commonly called the Eastern question. Since Europeans approved the book, Americans at once bought and discussed it; to prove, I suppose, that as a nation we are no longer tainted with provincialism,—as if that very subservience to transatlantic opinion were not the best proof that the virus still works within us. It was issued anonymously, through the fear that if I put my pseudonym on the title-page it might lead to inquiry about the author which would reveal his identity with Donald Maitland, for whom I only wished oblivion. As a result the question of authorship was much mooted, some declaring a well-known Oxford professor to be the man, others ascribing the volume to a famous German traveler, and Humzel being named by some; but most of the reviews suggested that it was the work of an Eastern savant, and I presume that my style was tinged with orientalism.

You cannot tell what a delight it was to me to learn, at our first meeting in the autumn, that you had read my book. I went in November to the Lenox Library to verify a date, and found you there. I could not help interrupting your reading for a moment,—I had so longed for a glimpse and a word,— and you took my intrusion in good part. I drew a book and pretended to read, merely to veil my covert watching of you; and when you rose to go, I asked permission to walk with you.

"Your notebook suggests that you are a writer by profession, Dr. Hartzmann?" you surmised.

"Yes."

"And you have to come to America for material?"

"I have come to America permanently."

"How unusual!"

"In what respect?"

"For a European writer to come to New York to do more than lecture about himself, have his vanity and purse fed, and return home to write a book about us that we alone read."

I laughed and said, "You make me very glad that I am the exception to the rule."

"I presume more would make the venture if they found the atmosphere less uncongenial. New York as a whole is so absorbed in the task of trans-shipping the products of the busiest nations of two continents that everything is ranked as secondary that does not subserve that end: and the Muses starve."

"I suppose New York is not the best of places in which to live by art or letters, if compared with London or Paris; yet if a man can do what the world wants done, he can earn a livelihood here."

"But he cannot gain the great prizes that alone are worth the winning, I fear. I have noticed that American writers only reach American audiences, while European authors not merely win attention at home, but have vogue and sale here. The London or Paris label is quite as effective in New York or Chicago in selling books as in selling clothes."

"I suppose cultivated Europe is as heedless of the newer peoples as the peoples of the Orient are of those of the Occident. Yet I think that if as good work were turned out in this country as in the Old World, the place of its production would not seriously militate against its success."

"And have you found it so?"

"Nothing I have yet written in this country merits Continental attention."

"I hope you have succeeded to your own satisfaction?"

"It may amuse you to know that though I had many good letters of introduction to editors in this country, I could not get a single article accepted till some friends of mine in Asia came to my aid."

"You speak in riddles."

"Perhaps you remember reading, last August, of an outbreak of some tribes in the Hindoo Kush? Those hill peoples are in a state of perennial ferment, and usually Europe pays no attention to their bellicose proceedings; but luckily for me, the English premier, at that particular moment, was holding his unwilling Parliament together in an attempt to pass something, and finding it intractable in that matter, he cleverly used this outbreak to divert attention and excite enthusiasm. Rising in the House of Commons, he virtually charged the outbreak to Russian machination against the beloved Emir, and pledged the nation to support that civilized humanitarian against the barbaric despot of Russia. At once the papers were full of unintelligible cablegrams telling of the doings in those far-away mountains; and my hurriedly written editorials and articles, which nevertheless showed some comprehension of the geography and people, were snapped up avidly, and from that time I have found papers or periodicals glad to print what I write."

You laughed, and said, "How strangely the world is tied together in these days, that the speech of an English prime minister about some Asian septs should give a German author entrée to New York editorial sanctums!"

"The cables have done more in aid of the brotherhood of man than all the efforts of the missionaries."

"I thought you were a conservative, and disapproved of modern innovations," you suggested archly.

"With innovators, yes."

"Then the Levantine does not entirely disapprove of our Hesperian city?"

"My knowledge of New York is about as deep," I answered, smiling, "as my Eastern blood."

"Only skin-deep," you said.

"Just sufficient for a disguise."

"As long as you are silent, yes."

"Is my English so unmistakable?"

"Not your tongue, but your thought. Of course your vicinage, costume, and complexion made me for a moment accept your joke of nationality, at that first meeting, but before you had uttered half your defense of the older races I felt sure that you were not a product of one of them."

"Why was that?"

"Because it is only Christians who recognize and speak for the rights of other peoples."

"You forget that the religion of Buddha is toleration. We Christians preach the doctrine, but practice extermination, forgiving our enemies after killing them," I corrected. "I do not think we differ much in works from even El Mahdi."

"Would El Mahdi ever have spoken for other races?"

"You know the weak spot in my armor, Miss Walton," I was obliged to confess.

"That is due to you, Dr. Hartzmann. What you stated that night interested me so deeply that I have been reading up about the Eastern races and problems. I wonder if you have seen this new book of travel, The Debatable Lands between the East and West?"

"Yes," I assented, thinking that twenty over-lookings of it in manuscript and proof entitled me to make the claim.

"You will be amused to hear that, when reading it, I thought of you as the probable writer, not merely because it begins in the Altai range and ends at Tangier, but as well because some of the ideas resemble yours. Mr. Whitely, however, tells me he has private information that Professor Humzel is the author. Do you know him?"

"He was my professor of history at Leipzig."

"That accounts for the agreement in thought. You admire the book?"

"I think it is a conscientious attempt to describe what the author saw."

"Ah, it is much more than that!" you exclaimed. "At a dinner in London, this autumn, I sat next the Earl—— next a member of the Indian Council, and he told me he considered it a far more brilliant book than Kinglake's Eothen."

I knew I had no right to continue this subject, but I could not help asking, "You liked it?"

"Very much. It seems to me a deep and philosophic study of present and future problems, besides being a vivid picture of most interesting countries and peoples. It made me long to be a nomad myself, and wander as the author did. The thought of three years of such life, of such freedom, seems to stir in me all the inherited tendency to prowl that we women supposedly get from Mother Sphinx."

"Civilization steals nature from us and compounds the theft with art."

"Tell me about Professor Humzel," you went on, "for I know I should like him, merely from the way he writes. One always pictures the German professor as a dried-up mind in a dried-up body, but in this book one is conscious of real flesh and blood. He is a young man, I'm sure."

"Sixty-two."

"He has a young heart, then," you asserted. "Is he as interesting to talk with as he makes himself in his book?"

"Professor Humzel is very silent."

"The people who have something to say are usually so," you sighed.

"A drum must be empty to make a noise," I said, smiling, "and perhaps the converse is true."

I cannot say what there was in that walk which cheered me so, except your praise of my book,—sweeter far though that was than the world's kindly opinion; yet over and above that, in our brief interchange of words, I was made conscious that there was sympathy between us,—a sympathy so positive that something like our old-time friendship seemed beginning. And the thought made me so happy that for a time my troubles were almost forgotten.

Good-night, Maizie.

XII

March 3. Fate seemed determined that our lives should be closely connected. In December Mr. Blodgett wrote asking me to call at his office, and he was already smiling when his boy passed me through the door at which so many had to tarry.

"There are a good many kinds of fools," was his welcoming remark, "but one of the commonest is the brand who think because they can do one thing well, they ought to be able to do the exact opposite. I've known men who could grow rich out of brewing beer, who kept themselves poor through thinking they knew all about horses; I've known women who queened it in parlors, who went to smash because they believed themselves inspired actresses; I've sat here in this office thirty years, and grown rich through the belief of clergymen, doctors, merchants, farmers,—the whole box and dice,—that they were heaven-born financiers, and could play us Wall Street men even at our own game. Whatever else you do in this world, doctor, don't think that because you can talk a dozen languages, they fit you to be a successful mute."

"When you are in this mood, Mr. Blodgett, I can be nothing else," I interpolated, as he paused a moment for breath.

"Alexander Whitely," he went on, smiling, "probably knows more about petroleum and kerosene than any other man in the world, and he's made himself rich by his knowledge. But it doesn't satisfy him to be on the top of his own heap; he wants to get on the top of some other fellow's. In short, he has an itch to be something he isn't, and the darned fool's gone and bought a daily newspaper with the idea that he is going to be a great editor!"

"His lamp of genius will not go out for want of oil," I remarked.

"For a moment he showed one glimmer of sense: he came to me for advice," said Mr. Blodgett in evident enjoyment. "I told him to get an A 1 business manager, to make you chief editor, let you pick your staff, and then blow in all the money you and the business end asked for, and never go inside the building himself. It was too good sense for him, for he's daft with the idea of showing the world how to edit a paper. But my advice simmered down to this: if you want to be his private secretary, at four thousand a year, and pretend to revise his editorials, but really write them for him, I guess you can have the position. Of course he is to think he writes the rubbish."

"A Voltaire in miniature," I laughed.

"A what?"

"The great Frederic thought himself a poet, and induced Voltaire to come and be his literary counselor. The latter showed a bundle of manuscripts to some one and sneered, 'See all this dirty linen of the king's he has sent me to wash.'"

"That was one for his nibs," chuckled Mr. Blodgett appreciatively. "But you mustn't make such speeches as that of Whitely."

"In spite of my many tongues, I can be mute."

"Do you think I haven't seen that? And I've seen something more, which is that you always give a dollar's worth of work for seventy-five cents of wages. Now, Whitely's a hard man, and if you made the terms with him he'd be sure to get the better of you. So I've arranged to have him meet you here, and I'm going to see fair play. I've told him you won't do it for less than four thousand, and he'll not get you a cent cheaper. The work will be very light."

"The work is easy," I assented, "but is it honest?"

"Seems to me we had better leave that to Whitely to settle."

"And is Mr. Whitely an honest man?"

Mr. Blodgett smiled as he looked at me, and observed, "Whitely wouldn't steal a red-hot stove unless it had handles! But he probably thinks this all right. Few people know how much successful men use other men's brains. Here's a report on a Southern railroad by an expert in my employ. I've never even been over the road, yet I'll sign my name to the report as if it was my work. Now, in oil Whitely hires all kinds of men to do different things for him, and he gets whatever credit follows; and I suppose he thinks that if he pays you to write editorials, they are as much his as any other thing he buys."

"He must be conscious of a distinction."

"That's his lookout, if he is. Don't start in to keep other people's consciences in order, doctor, for it's the hardest-worked and poorest-paid trade in the world."

When Mr. Whitely arrived, Mr. Blodgett was as good as his word, taking the matter practically out of my hands, and letting me sit a passive and amused spectator of the contest between the two shrewd men, who dropped all thought of personal friendship while they discussed the matter. Mr. Blodgett won, and made the further stipulation that since Mr. Whitely intended to be at the office only in the afternoon, I might be equally privileged as to my hours of attendance. His forethought and kindness did more, for his last speech to Mr. Whitely was, "Then it's understood that the doctor writes your letters and revises your editorials, but nothing else." And as soon as we were alone he intimated, "Remember that, or before you know it he'll be screwing you to death. Don't you write anything extra for him unless there's extra pay. Now, don't waste my time by thanks in business hours, but come in to-night to dinner, so as to let the boss and Agnes congratulate you."

My employment began the first of the year, at which time the paper came into the hands of its new proprietor; and it amuses me to recall him as he sat at his desk that first day, thrumming it nervously, and trying to dictate an editorial on The Outlook for the New Year. A more hopeless bit of composition I have seldom read, and four times it was rewritten as I built it into shape.

The man has no more sense of form than he has of English. Even worse, he is almost without ideas. It has become his invariable custom to remark to me suavely, as he takes his seat at his desk about two o'clock, "Dr. Hartzmann, possibly you can suggest a good subject for me to write about to-day?" And when I propose one, he continues: "That is satisfactory. Jot down what you think I had better say, while I run over my mail." An hour later I lay the typewritten sheets before him, and, after reading them with the most evident pleasure, he puts his initials at the top and sends the editorial out to the managing editor; to have a second pleasure when, after two hours, the galley slips of proof come back to him.

Fortunately for me, he cares no more for politics than I do, and thus saves me from the necessity of studying and mastering that shifting quicksand against which beat the tides of men, ebbing as private greed obtains the mastery, and flowing in those curious revulsions of selfishly altruistic public spirit called patriotism. Except for this subject his taste is catholic, and his foible is to pose as omniscient. "I wish new subjects,—something, if possible, that intellectual people do not know about,"—is his constant command; and nothing delights him more than an editorial on a subject of which he has never heard. Speaking only his mother tongue, he has an inordinate desire for foreign words, and will observe, "A quotation in another language gives an editorial page an air of culture which I desire my paper to have." Our composing-room, I imagine, is the only one in New York which has Greek type, and if I gave him the smallest encouragement he would buy fonts of Sanskrit and Hebrew characters. He always makes me teach him how to pronounce the sentences, catching them with a wonderful parrot-like facility. Usually he carries clippings of the last half dozen editorials with him, and his delight is to make an opportunity to read one aloud, prefaced by the announcement that he is the writer. Sometimes, indeed, he cannot contain his pleasure over the articles till their appearance in type, and I repeatedly hear him request a visitor, "If you have ten minutes to spare, let me read you this editorial I have just written for to-morrow's issue."

At first, in spite of Mr. Blodgett's explanation, I thought this real dishonesty, and despised not merely him, but myself as well for aiding in such trickery. As I grow to know him better, however, I find he is not cozening the public so much as imposing on himself. The man has a fervent and untrained imagination, which has never, in the practicalities of oil, had a safety-valve. As a result, it has rioted in dreams of which he is the hero, until it has brought him to the point of thinking his wildest fancies quite possible realities. His self-faith is so great that his imagination sets no limit to his powers, and thus he can believe everything of himself. I have heard him tell what he would do under given circumstances, and, with my knowledge of him, I know he is conceiving himself to be actually doing what he describes. Thus, in a smaller sense, he really imagines that he writes the editorials, and he even reads them to Mr. Blodgett, apparently unconscious that there can be the slightest question of authorship in the latter's mind.

With this singular weakness the man is yet a strong one. His capacity to judge and manage men or facts is truly marvelous. He rules his paper as he rules everything, with the firmest hand, and not a man in his employ but knows who is master. Within a year he turned the journal into a great earner of money, and in the business office they have to confess that it is all his work, ignorant though he is to this day of the details. He knows by instinct where money should be spent, and where it should be scrimped. Yet with all this business shrewdness he cares not half so much that his investment is paying him twenty per cent as that people are talking about his ability as an editor, and my only influence over him even now is the praise my editorials have won him.

Perhaps the most singular quality of his nature is his heedlessness of individual opinion, and his dread of it in mass. He is so absolutely self-centred—every thought directed inward—that he never tries to make the individual like him, yet he craves intensely the world's esteem. He longs for notoriety, and even stoops to an almost daily mention of himself in his paper, taking endless pains to get his name into other journals as well. Even his philanthropy, for which the world admires him, is used for this purpose. Ridiculous as it may seem, the most grating task I have to do is the writing of the fulsome press dispatches which he invariably sends out whenever he makes one of his gifts. He writes, too, to his fellow editors, asking them to comment on the largess; and since he makes it a point to cultivate the pleasantest relations with his confrères, they give him good measure, though with many a smile and wink among themselves when they get together. "Mr. White-Lie" is his sobriquet in the fraternity.

How curiously diverse the same man is to different people! To the world Mr. Whitely is a man of great business ability, of wide knowledge, of great benevolence, and of fine manners. I do not wonder, Maizie, that he imposes on you; for though you have discernment, yet you are not of a suspicious nature, and his acting is so wonderful and his manner so frank, through his own unconsciousness of his self-deceit, that not a dozen people dream the man is other than he seems. You might, perhaps, in spite of his taciturnity, have discovered his charlatan pretense of learning if you had been born inquisitive, but you take his writings for the measure of his intellect, and have no more reason to suspect that his skillful reservations are the refuge of a sciolist than that my silence covers such little erudition as I have.

Why I can do naught else but sit here and write of the past I do not understand. Until a month ago I was working every evening till far into the night, but now, try as I may, I can no longer force myself to my task. I should think it was physical exhaustion, were it not that I can chronicle this stale record of what I know so well. I suppose it is mental discouragement at my slight progress in reducing that crushing debt, and, even more, my sadness at the thought of you as his wife.

Good-night, my darling. May happiness be yours.

XIII

March 4. My impressions of that first winter in New York are curiously dim except for the extreme loneliness of my life, which, after the close companionship with my father for so many years, seemed at times almost unbearable. Indeed, I doubt if I could have borne the long hours of solitude and toil but for my occasional glimpses of you. I should think myself fatuous in claiming that you influence me physically,—that I am conscious of a material glow, ecstasy, thrill, call it what you please, when with you,—if I had not once heard Agnes declare that she always felt, when you were in the room, as if she had been drinking champagne; showing that I am not the only one you can thus affect.

My pleasantest recollection is of our long talk in my employer's study; and strangely enough, it was my books which gained it for me. Mr. Whitely, when I first came into his service, had just endowed a free library in one of the Western cities where some of his oil interests centred, and I hinted to him the purchase of my books as a further gift to his hobby. The suggestion did not meet with his approval,—I fear because there was not the self-advertising in it that there is in a money gift,—but after a week he told me that he might buy the collection to furnish his editorial study. "I plan," he said, "to make my office attractive, and then have informal literary receptions once a week. I shall therefore require some books, and as your library should be marked by breadth and depth of learning, I presume it will serve my purpose."

"There are quite a number of Eastern manuscripts of value," I told him, "and few of the books are in languages that can be read by the average New Yorker."

"That gives the suggestion of scholarship which I wish," he acknowledged.

We easily came to terms under these circumstances, and I cannot tell you how happy I was to find myself once more surrounded by my books. As soon as they were in place and the study was handsomely furnished, my employer issued cards; and though he had nothing in common with the literary and artistic set, the mere fact that he controlled the columns of a great paper brought them all flocking to his afternoons. It is a case of mutual cultivation, and I am sick of being told to write puffs of books and pictures. Even foreigners do not seem above this log-rolling, and toady to the editor of the influential journal. And yet we think Johnson mean-spirited for standing at Chesterfield's door! It humiliates me to see writers and artists stooping so low merely to get notices that are worthless in a critical sense, and doubly am I degraded that mine is the pen that aids in this contemptible chicane.

You, Mrs. Blodgett, and Agnes came to one of these afternoons, and made me happy, not alone by your presence, but by an insinuated reproof, which meant, I thought, that you had become enough interested in me to care what I did. You expressed surprise at my being there, and so I explained to you that I had become Mr. Whitely's secretary.

"And is your work congenial?" you asked.

I shrugged my shoulders, and quoted, "Civilized man cannot live without dining."

"But you told me you were making a living. Is not a crust with independence and a chance to make a name better than such work?"

"If one is free, yes. But if one must earn money?"

"I had somehow fixed it in my mind that you were *en garçon*. One's fancies are sometimes very ridiculous. Who invented the mot that a woman's intuitions were what she had when she was wrong?"

"Some man, of course," I laughed. "And you were right in supposing me a bachelor."

"How little people really know about one another," you observed, "and yet we talk of the realism of life! I believe it is only in fiction that we get it."

"Napoleon said, 'Take away history and give me a novel: I wish the truth!' Certainly, our present romance writers attempt it."

"Only to prove that truth is not art."

"How so?"

"To photograph life in literature is no more art than a reproduction of our street sounds would be music."

"Painting and sculpture are copying."

"And the closer the copy, the less the art."

"Then you would define art as"—

"The vivifying of work with the personality of the workman."

"That is not very far from Saadi's thought that art is never produced without love."

"I have to confess that you mention an author of whom I had never even heard till I read The Debatable Lands. The extracts printed there made me think he must be one of the great philosopher poets of the world. Yet there is no copy of his works at the Lenox."

"There are copies of all his writings here."

"I think I shall disobey Polonius by trying to be a borrower," you announced, and turning to Mr. Whitely, you asked, "Do you ever loan your books?"

"To lend to you would be a pleasure, and give added value to the volume," assented Mr. Whitely, joining us. "Take anything you wish."

"Thank you so much. Will you let me see what you have of Saadi, so that I may take my choice?"

"You were speaking of"—hemmed Mr. Whitely.

"Saadi."

"Ah, yes. Dr. Hartzmann knows where it is."

When I had led the way to the proper shelf, you selected the Gulistan, opened it, and then laughed. "You have the best protection against borrowers. I envy both of you the ability to read him in the original, but it is beyond me."

"As you read Latin, you can read Gentius' translation of the Bostan," I suggested, taking the book down.

"How do you know that I can read Latin?" you asked.

I faltered for a moment, too much taken aback to think what to reply, and fortunately Mr. Whitely interposed quickly, "Miss Walton's reputation for learning is so well recognized that knowledge of Latin is taken for granted."

Taking advantage of the compliment, I surmised, "Perhaps you will care less to read the poet if I quote a stanza of his:—

> 'Seek truth from life, and not from books, O fool!
> Look at the sky to find the stars, not in the pool.'"

"You only make me the more eager," you said, running over the pages.

"The book is worth reading," vouched Mr. Whitely.

"How good that is!" you appealed to him, laying your finger on lines to the effect that a dozen poor men will sleep in peace on a straw heap, while the greatest empire is too narrow for two kings.

"Very," answered my employer, after looking at the text with a critical air. If you could only have enjoyed the joke with me!

Suddenly, as I watched you, you became pale, and glancing down to learn the cause, I saw a manuscript note in my father's handwriting on the margin of the page. "Mr. Whitely," you asked huskily, "how did you get this book?"

Had you looked at me you would have seen one paler than yourself, as I stood there expecting the axe to fall. Oh! the relief when Mr. Whitely replied, "I bought it in Germany."

You closed the volume, remarking, "I do not think I will ask the loan, after all. He seems an author one ought to own."

"I hoped you would add an association to the book," urged Mr. Whitely.

"Thank you," you parried gravely, "but so old a volume can hardly be lacking in association. I think we must be going."

I took you down to the carriage, and Mrs. Blodgett kindly offered me the fourth seat. You were absolutely silent in the drive up-town, and I was scarcely less so as I tried to read your thoughts. What feelings had that scrap of writing stirred in you?

I have often since then recalled our parting words that afternoon, and wondered if I allowed a mere scruple—a cobweb that a stronger man would have brushed aside without a second thought—to wreck my life. If I had taken what you offered? Perhaps the time might have come when I could have told you of my trick, and you would have forgiven it. Perhaps—

You said to me graciously, when we separated at your door, "I shall be very happy, Dr. Hartzmann, if you will come to see me."

I flushed with pleasure, for I felt it was not a privilege you gave to many. But even as I hesitated for words with which to express my gratitude, I realized that I had no moral right to gain your hospitality by means of my false name; and when I spoke it was to respond, "I thank you for the favor most deeply, Miss Walton, but I am too busy a man for social calls."

Oh, my darling, if you had known what those few words cost me, and the struggle it was to keep my voice steady as I spoke them! For I knew you could only take them to mean that I declined your friendship. Hide my shame as I might try to do, I could not escape its pains. God keep you from such suffering, Maizie, and good-night.

XIV

March 5. Though I committed the rudeness of refusing to call, you never in our subsequent intercourse varied your manner by the slightest shade, treating me always with a courtesy I ill deserved. After such a rebuff, it is true, you were too self-respecting to offer me again any favor tending to a better acquaintance, but otherwise you bore yourself towards me as you did towards the thousand other men whom you were obliged to meet.

Your life as a social favorite, and mine as a literary hack, gave little opportunity for our seeing each other, yet we met far more frequently than would have seemed possible. Occasionally I found you at the Blodgetts', though not as often as our informal footing in that household had led me to hope; for you were in such social demand that your morning hours were the time you usually took to run in upon them. But now and then we lunched or dined there, and Mrs. Blodgett little dreamed how willingly I obeyed her positive command that I was to come to every one of her afternoons when Agnes told me that you were to receive or pour tea. Little I had of your attention, for you were a magnet to many, but I could stand near you and could watch and listen, and that was happiness.

A cause of meeting more discordant to me was furnished by my employer. I wrote for him an editorial on the folk-leid basis of the Wagner trilogy, which I suppose he sent or read to you; for it resulted in a box-party to attend the series, and I was asked to be one of the guests. "Nothing like having your books of reference under your arm," was Mr. Whitely's way of telling me for what purpose I was wanted; and I presume that was, in truth, the light in which he viewed me. Though I scorned such service, the mere fact that you were to be there was enough to make me accept. How low love can bring a man if his spirit is once mastered by it!

I would have sunk far deeper, I believe, to obtain what I earned, for there were delightful moments of mutually absorbing discussions, only too quickly interrupted by Mr. Whitely or others of the party breaking in on our conversation. What was equal happiness to me was the association of you in my mind with the noblest of music. I can never hear certain movements of those operas without your image coming before me as clearly as if I saw your reflection in a mirror. And from that time one of my keenest pleasures has been to beg tickets from the musical critic of our staff, whenever one of the trilogy is to be given, and sit through the opera dreaming of those hours. I could write here every word you uttered, but what especially impressed itself upon my memory was something called out by the fate of Brunhilde. As we stood in the lobby waiting for the carriages, at the end of Die Walküre, you withdrew a little, as if still feeling the beauty and tragedy of the last act too deeply to take part in the chit-chat with which the rest of the party beguiled the time. I stood near you, but, respecting your mood, was silent too, until you finally broke the pause by saying, "I do not know whether it is Wagner's music or because Brunhilde appeals to me, but I always feel that I have suffered as she does. It almost makes me believe in the theory of metempsychosis."

"Is it so much consciousness of a past, Miss Walton," I suggested, "as prescience of the future? Woman's story is so unvaryingly that of self-sacrifice for love that I should suppose Brunhilde's fate would appeal to the sex as a prophecy rather than as a memory."

"Her punishment could have been far worse."

"Left a defenseless prey to the first comer?"

"But surrounded by fire, so that the first comer must be a brave man."

"Do you value courage so highly?"

"Yes. The truly brave, I think, cannot be mean, and without meanness there must be honor. I almost envy Brunhilde her walls of fire, which put to absolute proof any man who sought her. The most successful of men; the most intellectually brilliant, may be—By what can we to-day test courage and honor?"

"There is as much as ever, Miss Walton. Is it no gain that courage has become moral rather than physical?"

"Is it no loss that of all the men I know, there is not one of whom I can say with certainty, 'He is a brave man'?"

Our numbers were called at this point, and the conversation was never continued. Every word you had said recalled to me my former friend, and I understood your repugnance for anything cowardly.

At the last of these operas, by another perverse joke of Dame Fortune, who seems to have so many laughs at my expense, I was introduced to the chaperon, "Mrs. Polhemus." Looking up, I found myself facing my mother. I cannot tell you how strangely I felt in making my bow. She was as handsome as ever, it appeared to me, and the smooth rich olive complexion seemed to have given her an undying youth. For a moment I feared recognition, but the difference was too great between the pallid stooping boy of fifteen she had last seen in Paris and the straight bronzed man of twenty-seven. As of old she was magnificently dressed and fairly glittered with diamonds, which curiously enough instantly brought to my mind the face of my father as I kissed him last. Was it the strong connection of contrast, or was it a quirk of my brain?

This chance meeting had a sequel that pains me to this day. Dining the next evening at the Blodgetts' with you and your uncle, the latter spoke of my mother's diamonds. Mrs. Blodgett said, with a laugh, "One would think, after her rich marriage, that she might pay up the money her first husband stole from Maizie."

"She could have done that years ago if she had cared to," sneered Mr. Walton.

Your eyes were lowered, and you still kept them so as you replied, "I would not accept the money from Mrs. Polhemus."

In my suffering I sat rigid and speechless, wincing inwardly at each blow of the lash, when Mr. Blodgett, with a kindness I can never reward or even acknowledge, observed, "I believe it was his wife's extravagance which made William Maitland a bankrupt and an embezzler. Till his marriage with her he was a man of simple habits and of unquestioned business honesty, but he was caught by her looks, just as Polhemus has been. In those first years he could deny her nothing, and when the disillusionment came he was too deep in to prevent the wreck."

"You've been revising your views a bit," retorted Mr. Walton. "I never expected to hear you justify any of that family."

"Perhaps I have reason to," replied Mr. Blodgett.

"I don't believe any of those Maitlands have the least honesty!" exclaimed Agnes. "How I hate them!"

"It is not a subject of which I like to speak," you stated in an evidently controlled voice, still with lowered eyes, "but it is only right to say that some one—I suppose the son—is beginning to pay back the debt."

"Pay back the money, Maizie!" ejaculated Mr. Walton. "Why haven't you told me of it?"

"It did not seem necessary," you answered.

"I'm sure it's a trick," asserted Agnes. "He's probably trying to worm his way back to your friendship, to get something more out of you."

"How much"—began Mr. Walton; but you interrupted him there by saying, "I would rather not talk about it."

The subject was changed at once, but when we were smoking, Mr. Walton asked, "Blodgett, do you know anything about that Maitland affair?"

"A little," replied the host.

"The debt really is being paid?"

"Yes."

"And you don't know by whom?"

"So Maizie tells me."

"Has she made no attempt to find out?"

"When the first payment was made she came to me for advice."

"Well?" asked Mr. Walton eagerly.

"She got it," declared Mr. Blodgett.

"What did she do?" persisted Mr. Walton.

Mr. Blodgett was silent for a moment, and then responded, "The exact opposite of what I advised. Do you know, Walton, you and I remind me of the warm-hearted elephant who tried to hatch the ostrich eggs by sitting on them."

"In what respect?"

"We decided that we must break up Maizie's love of the Maitlands for her own good."

"Well?"

"Well, we made the whole thing so mean to her that finally we did break something. Then, manlike, we were satisfied. What was it we broke?"

"Nonsense!" growled Mr. Walton, sipping his wine.

Mr. Blodgett laughed slightly. "That's rather a good name for it," he assented; "but the trouble is, Walton, that nonsense is a very big part of every woman's life. You'll never get me to fool with it again."

I often ponder over those three brief remarks of yours, and of what you said to me last autumn, in our ride and in the upper hall of My Fancy, trying to learn, if possible, what your feeling is towards us. Can you, despite all that has intervened, still feel any tenderness and love for my father and me? Perhaps it was best that you were silent; if you had spoken of him with contempt, I think—I know you would not, my darling, for you loved him once, and that, to you, would be reason enough to be merciful to the dead, however sinning.

Dear love, good-night.

XV

March 6. You once said to me that you could conceive of no circumstances that would justify dishonesty; for, no matter what the seeming benefits might be, the indirect consequences and the effect on the misdoer's character more than neutralized them. The wrong I have done has only proved your view, and I have come to scorn myself for the dishonorable part I have played. Yet I think that you would pity more than blame me, if you could but know my sacrifices. I drifted into the fraud unconsciously, and cannot now decide at what point the actual stifling of my conscience began. I suppose the first misstep was when I entered Mr. Whitely's employment; yet though I knew it to be unscrupulous in him to impose my editorials as his own, it still seemed to me no distinct transgression in me to write them for him. With that first act those that followed became possible, and each involved so slight an increase in the moral lapse, and my debt to you was so potent an excuse to blind me, that at the time I truly thought I was doing right. I wonder what you would have done had you been in my position?

Mr. Blodgett's shrewdness in stipulating what work I was to do for Mr. Whitely quickly proved itself. One of the magazines asked my employer to contribute an article on The Future of Journalism. Handing me the letter, he said, "Dr. Hartzmann, kindly write a couple of thousand words on that subject."

"That surely is not part of my duty, Mr. Whitely," I had the courage to respond.

He looked at me quickly, and his mouth stiffened into a straight line. "Does that mean that you do not choose to do it?" he asked suavely.

My heart failed me at the thought that if I lost my position I might never get so good a one, and should drag my debt through life. For once thought of you made me cowardly. I answered, "I will write it, Mr. Whitely;" and he said, "I thank you," as if I had done him a favor.

I told Mr. Blodgett of the incident, that evening, with a wry face and a laugh over my bravery, and he was furious at me.

"Why, you—you"—he stuttered. "Haven't you learned yet that the man wouldn't part with you for anything? He's so stuck up over his editorials and what people say of them that he'd as soon think of discharging his own mother before she weaned him."

Not content with venting his anger on me, he came into the office the next day and told Mr. Whitely I should not be imposed on, and finally forced him to agree that I should receive whatever the review paid for the article.

After this I wrote several magazine articles for Mr. Whitely, and soon another development of our curious relations occurred. One afternoon he informed me, "The Library trustees request me to deliver an address at the dedication of the building. I shall be grateful for any suggestions you can make of a proper subject."

"Books?" I replied, with an absolutely grave face.

"That is eminently suitable," he responded. "Possibly you can spare the time to compose such a paper; and as it should be of a scholarly character some Greek and Latin seem to me advisable."

"How much?" I asked, inwardly amused to note if he would understand my question, or would suppose it referred to the quantity of dead languages I was to inject.

"What is the labor worth?" he inquired, setting my doubt at rest, and proving his business ability to recognize the most distant allusion to a dollar. When I named a price, he continued: "That is excessive. The profession of authorship is so little recompensed that there are many good writers in New York who would gladly do it for less."

"I can do it cheaper, if, like them, I crib it from books at the Astor," I asserted.

"I do not see why an address composed in the Astor Library should not be entirely satisfactory?" he questioned, in his smooth, self-controlled manner.

"Did you never hear of the man who left the theatre in the middle of Hamlet because, he said, he didn't care to hear a play that was all quotations?" I asked, with a touch of irony.

"I presume the story has some connection in your mind with the subject in hand, but I am unable to see the appositeness?" he said interrogatively and evidently puzzled.

"I merely mentioned it lest you might not know that Pope never lived in Grub Street."

He looked at me, still ignorant that I was laughing at him. "You think it injudicious to have it done by Mather?" he questioned, naming a fellow who did special work for the paper at times.

"Not at all," I replied, "provided you label the address 'hash,' so that people who have some discrimination won't suppose you ignorant that it is twice-cooked meat you are giving them," and, turning, I went on with my work as if the matter were ended.

But the next day he told me, "I have concluded to have you compose that oration, Dr. Hartzmann;" and from that moment of petty victory I have not feared my employer.

I wrote the address, and it so pleased Mr. Whitely that, not content with delivering it, he had it handsomely printed, and sent copies to all his friends.

The resulting praise he received clearly whetted his appetite for authorship, for not long after he said to me, "Dr. Hartzmann, you told me, when you sold me this library, that you were writing a history of the Turks. How nearly completed is it?"

"I hope to have it ready for press within three months."

"For some time," he remarked, "I have meditated the writing of a book, and possibly yours will serve my purpose."

I was so taken by surprise that for a moment I merely gazed at him, since it seemed impossible that even egotism so overwhelming as his could be capable of such blindness; but he was in earnest, and I could only revert to Mr. Blodgett's idea that a business man comes to think in time that anything he can buy is his. I smiled, and answered, "My book is not petroleum, Mr. Whitely."

"If it is what I desire, I will amply remunerate you," he offered.

"It is not for sale."

"I presume," he replied, "that you know what disposition of your book suits you best. I have, however, noticed in you a strong desire to obtain money, and I feel sure that we could arrange terms that will bring you more than you would otherwise receive."

Even before Mr. Whitely finished speaking, I realized that I was not a free agent. I owed a debt, and till it was paid I had no right to think of my own ambition or feelings. I caught my breath in anguish at the thought, and then, fearing that my courage would fail me, I spoke hastily: "What do you offer me?"

He smiled blandly as he predicted: "It is hardly a work that will have a large sale. The Turkish nation has not played an important part in history."

"Only conquered the key of the Old World, caused the Crusades, forced the discovery of America and of the Cape passage, compelled Europe to develop its own civilization instead of adopting that of the East, and furnished a question to modern statesmen that they have yet found no Œdipus to answer," I retorted.

"Your special pleading does tend to magnify their position," he assented. "I shall be happy to look the work over, leaving the terms to be decided later."

I am ashamed to confess what a night of suffering I went through, battling with the love and pride that had grown into my heart for my book. I knew from the first moment his proposition had been suggested that he would give me more than I could ever hope to make from the work, and therefore my course was only too plain; but I had a terrible struggle to force myself to carry my manuscript to him the following afternoon.

For the next week he was full of what he was reading; and had the circumstances been different, I could have asked no higher compliment as regards its popular interest than the enthusiasm of this unlettered business man for my book.

"It is quite as diverting as a romance!" he exclaimed. "I can already see how astonished people will be when they read of the far-reaching influence of that nation."

Since the pound of flesh was to be sold, I took advantage of this mood. After much haggling, which irritated and pained me more than it should, Mr. Whitely agreed to give me six thousand dollars and the royalties. Good as the terms were, my heart nearly broke, the day the manuscript left my hands, for I had put so much thought into the book that it had almost become part of myself. My father, too, had toiled over it, with fondest predictions of the fame it would bring me; spending, as it proved, his very life in the endeavor to make it a great work. That his love, that the love of my dear professors, and that my own hopes should all be brought to market and sold as if they were mere merchandise was so mercenary and cruel that at the last moment it was all I could do to bring myself to fulfill the bargain. Nothing but my small progress in paying my debt would have forced me to sell, and I hope nothing but that would have led me to join in such dishonesty. It was, after all, part of the price I was paying for the original wrong, and but just retribution against which I had no right to cry out. Yet for a month I was so sad that I could scarcely go through my day's toil; and though that was a year ago, I have never been able to work with the same vim, life seems to have so little left in it for me. And idle as the thought is, when I think of your praise of the book I cannot help dreaming of what might have been if it had been published in my name; if—Ah, well, to talk of "ifs" is only to confess that I am beaten, and that I will not do. Nor is the fight over. I never hoped nor attempted to gain your love, and that he has won you does not mean failure. To pay my debt is all I have to do, and though I may feel more ill and disheartened than I do to-night, I will pay it, come what may.

Good-night, my darling.

XVI

March 7. It is little to be proud of, yet I like to think that though I have behaved dishonestly, I have not entirely lost my sense of right and wrong. Twice at least have I faced temptation and been strong enough to resist.

When I carried to Mr. Blodgett the money I received for my book, I was so profoundly discouraged that my mood was only too apparent. In his kindness he suggested that I buy certain bonds of a railroad his firm was then reorganizing,—telling me from his inside knowledge that a year's holding would give me a profit of thirty per cent. It was so sore a temptation to make money without exertion and practically without risk that I assented, and authorized him to buy the securities; but a night's reflection made the dishonesty of my act clear to me, and the next morning I went to his office and told him I wished to countermand my order.

"What's that for?" he inquired.

"I have thought better of the matter, and do not think I have the right."

"Why not?"

"If this money were a trust in my hands, it would not be honest to use it in speculation, would it?"

"No."

"That is practically what it is, since it was stolen from a trust, and is to be returned to it."

He smiled rather grimly. "It's lucky for Wall Street," he said, "that you literary fellows don't have the making and enforcing of laws; and it's luckier still that you don't have to earn your living down here, for the money you'd make wouldn't pay your burial insurance." Yet though he laughed cynically, he shook my hand, I thought, more warmly than usual when we parted, as if he felt at heart that I had done right.

Much easier to resist was an offer of another kind. Very foolishly, I told Mr. Whitely that I had received a letter from the literary editor of the leading American review asking if I would write the criticism of the History of the Turks.

"That is a singular piece of good fortune," Mr. Whitely said cheerfully, "and guarantees me a complimentary notice in a periodical that rarely praises."

"That is by no means certain," I answered. "You know as well as I that it does not gloze a poor book, nor pass over defects in silence."

"But you can hardly write critically of your own book!" cried Mr. Whitely, for once giving me a share in our literary partnership. "For if there are defects you ought to have corrected them in proof."

"Of course I do not intend to write the review!" I exclaimed.

"Not write it? Why not?" he questioned in amazement equal to mine.

"Because I am absolutely unfitted to do it."

"Why, you know all about the subject!"

"I mean that no author can for a moment write discriminatingly of his own work; and besides, the offer would never have been made if my connection with the book were known."

"But they will never know."

"I should."

"You mean to say you do not intend to do it?"

"I shall write to-night declining."

"But I want you to do it."

"And I don't."

"What would they probably pay you for it?"

"What it is worth."

"If you will reconsider your determination, I will double the amount."

"Unfortunately," I laughed bitterly, "there are limits to what even *I* will sell."

"I will give you two hundred and fifty dollars if you will write a laudatory review of my book," he offered.

"Have you ever dealt in consciences, Mr. Whitely?" I asked.

"Occasionally."

"Did you ever get any as cheap as that?"

"Many."

"I'm afraid you were buying shopworn and second-hand articles," I retorted; "or you may have gone to some bargain counter where they make a specialty of ninety-eight and forty-nine cent goods."

He never liked this satirical mood into which he sometimes drove me. He hesitated an instant, and then bid, "Three hundred."

"This reminds me of Faust," I remarked; but he was too intent on the matter in hand to see the point.

"I suppose it's only a question of amount?" he suggested blandly.

"You are quite right, Mr. Whitely. I will write you that review if you will pay me my price," I assented.

"I knew it," he asserted exultingly. "But you are mistaken if you think I will pay any fancy price."

"Then it's a waste of time to talk any more about it," I answered, and resumed my work.

"It isn't worth three hundred, even," he argued, "but you may tell me what you will do it for."

"I will write that review for one hundred and twenty-one thousand dollars," I replied.

"What!"

"And from that price I will not abate one cent," I added.

Strangely enough, I did not write the notice.

It was amusing to see his eagerness for the criticisms of the book. The three American critical journals had notices eminently characteristic of them. The first was scholarly, praising moderately, with a touch of lemon-juice in the final paragraph that really only heightened its earlier commendation, but which made the book's putative author wince; the second was discriminating and balanced, with far more that was complimentary; while the third was the publisher's puff so regularly served up,—a colorless, sugary mush,—which my employer swallowed with much delectation. I am ashamed to say that I greatly enjoyed his pain over any harsh words. He always took for granted that the criticisms were correct, never realizing that as between an author, who has spent years on a book, and the average critic, who is at best superficial in his knowledge of a subject, the former is the more often right of the two. I tried to make this clear to him one day by asking him if he had never read Lord Brougham's review of Byron or Baron Jeffrey's review of Coleridge, and even brought him the astonishing tirades of those world-renowned critics; but it was time wasted. He preferred a flattering panegyric in the most obscure of little sheets to a really careful notice which praised less inordinately; yet while apparently believing all the flattery, he believed all the censoriousness as well, even in those cases known to every author where one critic praises what another blames.

"A Western paper says you do not know how to write English," he complained one day. "You ought to have taken more pains with the book, Dr. Hartzmann."

"The Academy and The Athenæum both thought my style had merit," I answered, smiling.

"Nevertheless there must be something wrong, or this critic, who in other respects praises with remarkable discrimination, would certainly not have gone out of his way to mention it," he replied discontentedly.

Fortunately, unfavorable criticism, both in Europe and in America, was the exception, and not the rule; the book was generally praised, and sprang into an instant sale that encouraged and cheered me. Mr. Whitely was immensely gratified at the sudden reputation it achieved for him, and even while drinking deep of the mead of fresh authorship told me he thought he would publish another book. I knew it was an opportunity to make more money, but for some reason I felt unequal to beginning anew on what would be a purely mercenary task. I mentioned my plan of a work on the Moors, and promised, when I felt able to commence it, I would talk with him about terms. That was three months ago, yet every day I seem to feel less inclination, and in fact less ability, to undertake the labor. For three years I have toiled to the utmost of my strength, and forced myself to endure the most rigid economy. It is cowardly, but at times I find myself hoping my present want of spirit and energy is the forerunner of an illness which will end the hopeless struggle.

Good-night, dear heart.

XVII

March 8. Each day I determine to spend my evening usefully, but try as I may, when the time comes I feel too weary to do good work, and so morbidly recur to these memories. I ought to fight the tendency, the more that in reverting to the past I seem only to dwell on its sadness, thus intensifying my own depression. Let me see if I cannot for one night write of the good fortune that has come to me in the last three years.

Pleased with the success of my book of travel and text-books, and knowing of my wish for work, the American publishers offered me the position of assistant editor of their magazine and reader of manuscripts. By hard work and late hours the task could be done in my mornings and evenings, allowing me to continue in Mr. Whitely's employ; so I eagerly accepted the position. I can imagine few worse fates than reading the hopeless and impossible trash that comes to every publisher; but this was not my lot, for I was to read only the manuscripts that had been winnowed of the chaff. Yet this very immunity, as it proved, nearly lost me an opportunity of trying to be of service to you.

Returning a bundle of stuff to the manuscript clerk one day, I saw "M. Walton, 287 Madison Avenue, New York City," in your handwriting, on the cover of a bulky pile of sheets on his desk. Startled, I demanded, "What is this?"

"It's a rejected manuscript I was on the point of wrapping to return," the clerk answered.

Opening the cover, I saw, "A Woman's Problem, a Novel, by Aimez Lawton." It needed little perception to detect your name in the anagram.

"Mrs. Graham has rejected it?" I asked, and he nodded.

"Give me the file about it, please," I requested; and after a moment's search he handed me the envelope, and I glanced over its meagre contents: a brief formal note from you, submitting it, and the short opinion of the woman reader. "Traces of amateurishness, but a work of considerable power and feeling, marred by an inconclusive ending," was the epitome of her opinion, coupled with the recommendation not to accept.

"Register it on my list, and I'll take it and look it over," I said, and went to my little editorial cuddy, feeling actually rich in the possession of the manuscript. Indeed, it was all I could do to go through my morning quota of proof-reading and "making up" dummy forms for the magazine's next issue, I was so eager for your book.

A single reading told me you had put the problem of your life into the story. It is true the heroine was different enough in many respects to make analogy hardly perceptible, though she too was a tender, noble woman. She had never felt the slightest responsive warmth for any of her lovers, but she was cramped by the social conventions regarding unmarried women, and questioned whether her life would not be more potent if she married, even without love. One of her lovers was a man of force, brains, wealth, and ambition, outwardly an admirable match, respected by the world, and, most of all, able to draw about him the men of genius and intellect she wished to know, but whom her society lot debarred her from meeting. Yet your heroine was conscious of faults: she felt in him a touch of the soil that repels every woman instinctively; at times his nature seemed hard and unsympathetic, and his scientific work, for which he was famous, had narrowed his strong mind to think only of facts and practicalities, to the exclusion of everything ideal or beautiful. In the end, however, his persistent wooing convinced her of the strength of his feeling; and though she was conscious that she could never love him as she wished to love, the tale ended by her marrying him. Am I to blame for reading in this the story of Mr. Whitely's courtship of you? I only marveled at how much of his true character you had detected under his veneer.

To me the story was sweet and noble. I loved your heroine from beginning to end. She was so strong even in her weaknesses; for you made her no unsubstantial ideal. I understood her craving something more than her allotted round of social amusements, and her desire for intercourse and friendship with finer and more purposeful people than she daily met. I even understood her willingness to accept love, when not herself feeling it; for my own life was so hungry-hearted that I had come to yearn for the slightest tenderness, no matter who the giver might be.

As soon as I realized that the story was your own, I hoped it might tell me something of your thoughts of my father and myself; but that part of your life you passed over as if it never had been. Was the omission due to too much feeling or too little? I have always suspected that I served as a model for one of your minor characters: a dreamy, unsocial being, curiously variable in mood; at times talking learnedly and even wittily, but more often absolutely silent. He was by profession an artist, and you made him content to use his talent on book and magazine illustration, apparently without a higher purpose in life than to earn enough to support himself, in order that he might pass the remainder of his time in an intellectual indulgence scarcely higher in motive than more material dissipation. His evident sadness and lack of ambition was finally discovered to be due to a disappointment in love; and as a cure, your heroine introduced him to her best friend,—a young girl,—and through her influence he was roused to some ambition, and in the end he dutifully fell in love as your heroine wished. It was a sketch that made me wince, and yet at which I could not help but laugh. I suppose it was a true picture, and I am quite conscious that at times I must seem ridiculous to you; for often my mood is such, or my interest in you is so strong, that I forget even the ordinary courtesies and conventions. There is a general idea that a lover is always at his best when with the woman he loves, but, from my own experience, I think he is quite as likely to be at his worst. To watch your graceful movements, to delight in the play of expression on your face, and to catch every inflection in your voice and every word you speak are pleasures so engrossing to me that I must appear to you even more abstracted than I ordinarily am, though a dreamer at best. And yet now and then I have thought you were conscious of a tenderness in me, which, try as I will, I cannot altogether hide.

The main fault of the novel was unquestionably that most accented by the reader, and, recognizing the story as the problem of your life, I understood why you supplied no solution to the riddle. You begged the question you propounded; the fact that your heroine married the hero being no answer, since only by the results of that marriage would it be possible to say if she had chosen the better part. It was this that convinced me you were putting on paper your own thoughts and mood. You were debating this theme, and could carry it in imagination to the point of marriage; but what lay beyond that was unknowable, and you made no attempt to invent a conclusion, the matter being too real to you to be merely a subject for artistic idealism and invention. Hitherto I had classed Mr. Whitely with your other lovers, feeling sure that you could not love him any more than you could any of them; but now for the first time I began to fear his success.

After reading the story three times I carried it back to the manuscript clerk; and when I had allowed sufficient time for it to be returned, I wrote you a long letter, telling how I had come to read the story, and making a careful criticism and analysis of both its defects and its merits. I cannot tell you what a labor of love that letter was, or how much greater pains I took over your book than I have ever taken over any writing of my own. What was perhaps unfair, after pointing out the inconclusiveness of your ending, I sketched what I claimed was the logical end to the story. Thinking as I did that I knew the original in your mind, I was more influenced by my knowledge of him than I was by the character in your book, and therefore possibly my inference was unjust. But in hopes of saving you from Mr. Whitely, I pictured a sequel in which your heroine found only greater loneliness in her loveless union, her husband's love proving a tax, and not a boon; and marriage, instead of broadening her life, only bent and narrowed it by just so much as a strong-willed and selfish man would inevitably cramp the life of one over whom law and public opinion gave him control.

I was richly rewarded by your letter of thanks. You were so winning in your sweet acceptance of all my criticisms, and so lovable in your simple gratitude, that I would have done a thousand times the work to earn such a letter. Yet even in this guerdon I could not escape the sting of my unhappy lot; for, unable to reconcile my distant conduct with the apparent trouble I had taken, you asked me to dinner, leaving me to select the day, and spoke of the pleasure it would give you to have an opportunity to talk over the book with me.

I can think of few greater delights than to have gone over your story, line by line and incident by incident. My love pleaded with me to take the chance, pointing out that it would do you no harm, but on the contrary aid you, and I found a dozen specious reasons; but tempt me as they might, I always came back to the truth that if you knew who I really was you would not invite me, nor accept a favor at my hands. In the end I wrote you that my time was so mortgaged that I must deny myself the pleasure. A small compensation was my offer that if you chose to rewrite the story and send me the manuscript, I would gladly read it over again and make any further suggestions which occurred to me. You thanked me by letter gracefully, but I was conscious of your bewilderment in the very care with which you phrased your note; and when next we met I could see that I had become more an enigma than ever,—for which there is indeed small wonder.

God keep you, my darling.

XVIII

March 9. What seemed my misfortune proved quite the reverse. You evidently mentioned to Agnes my refusing to dine with you, and the next time I saw her she took me to task for it.

"It's too bad of you," she told me, "when I have explained to you how sensitive Maizie is, and how she has the idea that nice men do not like her, that you should go and confirm her in the feeling by treating her so! Why don't you like her?"

"I do," was all I said.

"No, you don't," she denied indignantly. "I suppose men dislike fine women because they make them feel what poor things they are themselves!"

"I like you, Miss Blodgett," I replied.

"I don't believe it," she retorted, "or you would be nice to my best friend. Besides, the idea of mentioning me in the same breath as Maizie! Men are born geese."

"Then you should pity rather than upbraid us," I suggested.

"I'll tell you what I intend to do," went on Agnes. "You promised us a visit this summer, and I am going to arrange for Maizie to be there at the time, so that you can really get to know her. And then, if you don't like her, I'll never forgive you."

"Now, Agnes," ordered Mrs. Blodgett crossly, "stop teasing the doctor. I'm fond of Maizie, but I'm fairly tired with men falling in love with her, and I am glad to find one who hasn't."

All last spring and summer, as I toiled over the proof sheets of my history, I was waiting and dreaming of that promised fortnight with you. I was so eager in my hope that when I found Agnes at the station, it was all I could do not to make my greeting a question whether you were visiting them. Luckily, she was almost as eager as I was, and hardly was I seated in the trap when she announced,—

"Mamma wanted to ask you when we were alone, and wouldn't hear at first of even Maizie being with us; but I told papa of my plan, and he insisted that Maizie should be invited. Wasn't he an old love? And now, Dr.

Hartzmann, you'll try to like Maizie, won't you? And even if you can't, just pretend that you do, please."

If the groom had not mounted the rumble at this point, I believe I should have told her of my love for you, the impulse was so strong, in my gratitude and admiration for the unselfish love she had for you.

A result of this misunderstanding was an amusing game of cross-purposes between mother and daughter. Agnes was always throwing us together, scarcely attempting to veil her wishes, while Mrs. Blodgett, thinking that I did not care for you, was always interfering to save me from your society. She proposed that I should teach Agnes chess, and left us playing; but when you joined us, Agnes insisted that she could learn more by watching us, only to play truant the moment you had taken her place. I shall never forget Mrs. Blodgett's amazement and irritation, on her return, at finding us playing, and Agnes not to be seen. Equally unsuccessful was an attempt to teach Agnes fencing, for she grew frightened before the foils had really been crossed, and made you take her place. At first I imagined she only pretended fear, but Mrs. Blodgett became so very angry over her want of courage that I had to think it genuine. When we went to drive as a party there was always much discussion as to how we should sit; and in fact my two friends kept at swords' points most of the time, in their endeavors to make me tolerate or save me from the companionship of the woman I loved. Even I could see the comedy of the situation.

In one of our conversations you reverted to your novel, and questioned my view of the impossibility of the heroine being happy in her marriage, evidently influenced, but not convinced, by my opinion.

"To me it is perfectly conceivable," you argued, "that, regardless of her loving, a woman can be as happy married as single, and that it all depends upon what she makes of her own life."

"But in marriage," I contended, "she is not free to make her life at all."

"Surely she is if her husband truly loves her."

"Less so than if he does not."

"You are not in earnest?"

"Yes. Love makes women less selfish, but with many men it often has the opposite effect. The man you drew, Miss Walton, was so firm that he would not be other than selfish, and if my reading of your heroine is correct, she was a woman who would resign her own will, rather than lower her self-respect by conflicts with her husband."

"But he loved her."

"In a selfish man's way. If women knew better what that meant, there would be fewer unhappy marriages."

"Then you are sure my heroine did wrong?"

"I think she did what thousands of other women have done,—she married the love rather than the lover."

"No. I did not intend that. She married for quite other things than love: for greater freedom, for"—

"Would she have married," I interrupted, "if she had not been sure that the hero loved her?"

You thought an instant, and then said, "No, I suppose not—and yet"— You stopped, and then continued impulsively, "I wonder if I shall shock you very much if I say that I have no faith in what we call love?"

"You do not shock me, Miss Walton, because I do not believe you."

"It is true, nevertheless. Perhaps it is my own fault, but I have never found any love that was wholly free from self-indulgence or self-interest."

"If you rate love so low, why did you make your heroine crave it?"

"One can desire love even when one cannot feel it."

"Does one desire what one despises?"

"To scorn money does not imply a preference for poverty."

"The scorn of money is as genuine as your incapacity to love, Miss Walton."

"You do not believe me?"

"A person incapable of love does not crave it. It is only a loving nature which cares for love."

"But if one cannot love, how can one believe in it?"

"The unlighted torch does not believe in fire."

"But some substances are incombustible."

"The sun melts anything."

"The sun is trans-terrestrial."

"So is love."

You looked at me in silence for a moment, and then asked, "Is love so much to you?"

"Love is the only thing worth striving for in this life," I replied.

"And if one fails to win it?"

"One cannot fail, Miss Walton."

"Why not?"

"Because the best love is in one's own heart and depends only on one's self."

"And if one has loved," you responded hurriedly, with a mistiness in your eyes which proved how deeply you were feeling, "if one gives everything— only to find the object base—if"—You stopped speaking and looked away.

"One still has the love, Miss Walton; for it is that which is given, and not that which is received, that is worth the having." I faltered in my emotion, and then, almost unconscious of what I said, went on: "For many years I have loved,—a love from the first impossible and hopeless. Yet it is the one happiness of my present life, and rather than"—I recovered control of myself, and became silent as I heard Mrs. Blodgett coming along the veranda.

You leaned forward, saying softly, "Thank you for the confidence." Then, as Mrs. Blodgett joined us, you said, "I envy you your happiness, Dr. Hartzmann."

"What happiness is that?" asked Mrs. Blodgett, glancing from one to the other curiously.

"Dr. Hartzmann," you explained calmly, without a trace of the emotion that had moved you a moment before, "has been proving to me that all happiness is subjective, and as I have never been able to rise to such a height I am very envious of him."

"I don't know what you mean," remarked Mrs. Blodgett. "But if the doctor wants to know what real happiness is, he had better marry some nice girl and have his own home instead of living in a boarding-house."

You laughed, and added, "Now our happiness becomes objective. Perhaps it is the best, after all, Dr. Hartzmann."

"Do *you* think so, Miss Walton?" I asked, unable to prevent an emphasis in the question.

You rose, saying, "I must dress for dinner." But in the window you turned, and answered, "I have always thought it was, but there are evident exceptions, Dr. Hartzmann, and after what you have told me I think you are one of them."

"And not yourself?" I could not help asking.

You held up your hand warningly. "When the nature of dolls is too deeply questioned into, they are found to contain only sawdust."

"And we often open the oyster, to find sometimes a pearl."

"The result of a morbid condition," you laughed back.

"Better disease and a pearl than health without it."

"But suppose one incapable of the ailment? Should one be blamed if no pearl forms?"

"An Eastern poet said:—

> Diving and finding no pearl in the sea,
> Blame not the ocean,—the fault is in thee.

Have you ever tried to find a pearl, Miss Walton?"

You hesitated a moment. "Like the Englishman's view of the conundrum," you finally parried archly, "that would be a good joke if there only wasn't something to 'guess' in it."

"Do you know what Maizie is talking about?" demanded Mrs. Blodgett discontentedly.

"Better than Miss Walton does herself, I think," I averred.

You had started to go, but again you turned, and asked with interest, "What *do* I mean?"

"That you believe what you think you don't."

You stood looking at me for a moment. "We are becoming friends, Dr. Hartzmann," you affirmed, and passed through the window.

Good-night, dear friend.

XIX

March 10. For the remainder of my visit, it seemed as if your prophecy of friendship were to be fulfilled. From the moment of my confidence to you, all the reserves that had been raised by my slighting of your invitations disappeared, perhaps because the secret I had shared with you served to make my past conduct less unreasonable; still more, I believe, because of the faith in you it evidenced in me. Certain I am that in the following week I felt able to be my true self when with you, for the first time since we were boy and girl together. The difference was so marked that you commented on the change.

"Do you remember," you asked me, "our conversation in Mr. Whitely's study, when I spoke of how little people really knew one another? Here we have been meeting for over three years, and yet I find that I haven't in the least known you."

It is a pleasure to me to recall that whole conversation, for it was by far the most intimate that we ever had,—so personal that I think I should but have had to question to learn what I long to know. In response to my slight assistance, to the sympathy I had shown, you opened for the moment your heart; willing, apparently, that I should fathom your true nature.

We had gone to dinner at the Grangers' merely to please Mrs. Blodgett, for we mutually agreed that in the country formal dinners were a weariness of the flesh; and I presume that with you, as with me, this general objection of ours was greatly strengthened when we found Mrs. Polhemus among the guests. It is always painful to me to be near her, and her dislike of you is obvious enough to make me sure that her presence is equally disagreeable to you. It is a strange warp and woof life weaves, that I owe to one for whom we both feel such repulsion the most sympathetic, the tenderest conversation I have ever had with you.

I was talking with Miss Granger, and thus did not hear the beginning of my mother's girds at you; but Agnes, who sat on my left, told me later that, as usual, Mrs. Polhemus set out to bait you by remarks superficially inoffensive, but covertly planned to embarrass or sting. The first thing which attracted my notice was her voice distinctly raised, as if she wished the whole table to listen, and in fact loud enough to make Miss Granger stop in the middle of a sentence and draw our attention to the speaker.

"—sound very well," Mrs. Polhemus was saying, "and are to be expected from any one who strives to be thought romantically sentimental."

"I did not know," you replied in a low voice, "that a 'romantically sentimental' nature was needed to produce belief in honesty."

"It is easy enough to talk the high morals of honesty," retorted your assailant, "and I suppose, Miss Walton, that for you it is not difficult to live up to your conversational ideals. But we unfortunate earthly creatures, who cannot achieve so rarefied a life, dare not make a parade of our ethical natures. The saintly woman is an enormously difficult rôle to play since miracles went out of style."

"Oh, leave us an occasional ideal, Mrs. Polhemus," laughed a guest. "I for one wish that fairy rings and genii were still the vogue."

"But we have some kinds of miracles," asserted Mrs. Granger. "Remember the distich,—

> 'God still works wonders now and then:
> Behold! two lawyers, honest men!'"

"With all due deference to Miss Walton's championing of absolute perfection," continued my mother, with a cleverly detached manner, to veil what lay back of the sneer, "I find it much easier to accept the miracle of an honest lawyer than that of an absolutely uncattish woman,"—a speech which, like most of those of Mrs. Polhemus, drew a laugh from the men.

"That's because you don't know Miss Walton!" exclaimed Agnes warmly, evidently fretted by such conduct towards you.

"On the contrary," answered my mother, speaking coolly and evenly, "I presume I have known Miss Walton longer and better than any one else in this room; and I remember when her views of honesty were such that her ideal was personified by a pair of embezzlers."

You had been meeting her gaze across the table as she spoke, but now you dropped your lids, hiding your eyes behind their long lashes; and nothing but the color receding from your cheeks, leaving them as white as your throat and brow, told of what you felt.

"Oh, say something," appealed Agnes to me in a whisper. "Anything to divert the"—

"And I really think," went on Mrs. Polhemus, smiling sweetly, with her eyes on you, "that if you were as thoroughly honest with us as, a moment ago, you were insistent on the world's being, you would confess to a *tendresse* still felt for that particular form of obliquity."

I shall recall the moment which followed that speech if it shall ever fall to me to sit in the jury-box and pass judgment on a murderer, for I know that had I been armed, and my mother a man, I should have killed her; and it taught me that murder is in every man's heart. Yet I was not out of my head, but was curiously clear-minded. Though allusion to my shame had hitherto always made me dumb, I was able to speak now without the slightest difficulty; I imagine because the thought of your pain made me forget my own.

"Which is better, Mrs. Polhemus," I asked, with a calmness I marveled at afterwards, "to love dishonesty or to dishonestly love?"

"Is this a riddle?" she said, though not removing her eyes from you.

"I suppose, since right and wrong are evolutionary," I rejoined, "that every ethical question is more or less of a conundrum. But the thought in my mind was that there is only nobility in a love so great that it can outlast even wrongdoing." Then, in my controlled passion, I stabbed her as deeply as I could make words stab. "Compare such a love, for instance, with another of which I have heard,—that of a woman who so valued the world's opinion that she would not get a divorce from an embezzling husband, because of the social stigma it involved, yet who remarried within a week of hearing of her first husband's death, because she thought that fact could not be known. Which love is the higher?"

The color blazed up in my mother's cheeks, as she turned from you to look at me, with eyes that would have killed if they could; and it was her manner, far more than even the implication of my words, which told the rest of the table that my nominally impersonal case was truly a thrust of the knife. A moment's appalling pause followed, and then, though the fruit was being passed, the hostess broke the terrible spell by rising, as if the time had come for the ladies to withdraw.

When, later, the men followed them, Agnes intercepted me at the door, and whispered, "Oh, doctor, it was magnificent! I was so afraid Maizie would break down if—I never dreamed you could do it so splendidly. You're almost as much of a love as papa! It will teach the cat to let Maizie alone! Now, do you want to be extra good?"

"So long as you don't want any more vitriol-throwing," I assented, smiling. "Remember that a hostess deserves some consideration."

"I told Mrs. Granger that you did it at my request, and there wasn't a woman in the room who didn't want to cheer. We all love Maizie, and hate Mrs. Polhemus; and it isn't a bit because you geese of men think she's handsome and clever, either. Poor Maizie wanted to be by herself, and went out on the veranda. I think she's had time enough, and that it's best for some one to go to her. Won't you slip out quietly?"

I nodded, and instantly she spoke aloud of the moon, and we went to the French window on the pretense of looking at it, where, after a moment, I left her. At first I could not discover you, the vines so shadowed your retreat; and when I did, it was to find you with bowed head buried in your arms as they rested on the veranda rail. The whole attitude was so suggestive of grief that I did not dare to speak, and moved to go away. Just as I turned, however, you looked up, as if suddenly conscious of some presence.

"I did not intend to intrude, Miss Walton, and don't let me disturb you. I will rejoin"—

"If you came out for the moonlight and quiet, sit down here," you said, making room for me.

I seated myself beside you, but made no reply, thinking your allusion to quiet perhaps voiced your own preference.

"It seems needless," you began, after a slight pause, "to ignore your kindness, even though it was veiled. I never felt so completely in another's power, and though I tried to—to say something—to strike back—I couldn't. Did my face so betray me that you knew I needed help?"

"Your face told nothing, it seemed to me."

"But that makes it positively uncanny. Over and over again you appear to divine my thoughts or moods. Do you?"

"Little more than any one can of a person in whom one is interested enough to notice keenly."

"Yet no one else does it with me. And several times, when we have caught each other's eyes, we have—at least I have felt sure that you were laughing with me, though your face was grave."

"Who was uncannily mind-reading then?"

"An adequate *tu quoque*," you said, laughing; then you went on seriously; "Still, to be frank, as now I think we can be, I have never made any pretense that I wasn't very much interested in you—while you—well—till very lately, I haven't been able to make up my mind that you did not actually—no, not dislike—for I knew that you—I could not be unconscious of the genuine esteem you have made so evident—yet there has always been, until the last two weeks, an indefinable barrier, of your making, as it appeared to me, and from that I could only infer some—I can give it no name."

"Were there no natural barriers to a friendship between a struggling writer and Miss Walton?"

"Surely you are above that!" you exclaimed. "You have not let such a distinction—Oh no, for it has not stood in the way of friendship with the Blodgetts."

A moment's silence ensued, and then you spoke again: "Perhaps there was a motive that explains it. Please don't reply, if it is a question I ought not to put, but after your confidence of last week I feel as if you had given me the privilege to ask it. I have always thought—or rather hoped—that you cared for Agnes? If'—

"And so you married me to her in the novel," I interrupted, in an effort to change the subject, dreading to what it might lead.

You laughed merrily as you said, "Oh, I'm so glad you spoke of that. I have often wondered if you recognized the attempted portrait,—which now I know is not a bit of a likeness,—and have longed to ask you. I never should have dared to sketch it, but I thought my pen name would conceal my criminality; and then what a fatality for you to read it! I never suspected you were the publisher's reader. What have you thought of me?"

"That you drew a very pleasant picture of my supposed mental and moral attainments, at the expense of my ambition and will. My true sympathy, however, went out to the girl whom you offered up as a heart-restorer for my earlier attachment."

"I'm thankful we are in the shadow," you laughed, "so that my red cheeks don't show. You are taking a most thoroughgoing revenge."

"That was the last thought in my mind."

"Then, my woman's curiosity having been appeased, be doubly generous and spare my absurd blushes. I don't know when I have been made to feel so young and foolish."

"Clearly you are no hardened criminal, Miss Walton. Usually matchmakers glory in their shame."

"Perhaps I should if I had not been detected, or if I had succeeded better."

"You took, I fear, a difficult subject for what may truly be called your maiden experiment."

"Did I not? And yet—You see I recognized potentialities for loving in you. You can—Ah, you have suggested to me a revenge for your jokes. Did you—were you the man who coined the phrase that my eyes were too dressy for the daytime?"

"Yes," I confessed guiltily, "but"—

"No, don't dare to try to explain it away," you ordered. "How could you say it? We can never be friends, after all."

Though you spoke in evident gayety, I answered gravely: "You will forgive me when I tell you that it was to parry a thrust of Mrs. Polhemus's at you, and I made a joke of it only because I did not choose to treat her gibe seriously. I hoped it would not come back to you."

"Every friend I have has quoted it, not once, but a dozen times, in my presence. If you knew how I have been persecuted and teased with that remark! You are twice the criminal that I have been, for at least my libel was never published. Yet you are unblushing."

We both sat silent for a little while, and then you began: "You interrupted a question of mine just now. Was it a chance or a purposed diversion? You see," you added hastily, "I am presuming that henceforth we are to be candid."

"I confess to an intention in the dodging, not because I feared the question, for a simple negative was all it needed, but I was afraid of what might follow."

"I hoped, after the trust of the other day—You do not want to tell me your story?"

"Are there not some things that cannot be put into words, Miss Walton? Could you tell me your story?"

"But mine is no mystery," you replied. "It has been the world's property for years. Why, your very help to-night proves that it is known to you,— that you know, indeed, facts that were unknown to me."

"Facts, yes; feelings, no."

"Do you appreciate the subtilty of the compliment? You really care for such valueless and indefinable things as feelings?"

"Yes."

"A bargain, then, while you are in this mood of giving something for nothing. Question for question, if you choose."

"You can tell your secrets?"

"To you, yes, for you have told me your greatest."

"Then, with the privilege of silence for both, begin."

"Ah, you begin already to fear the gimlet! Yes. Nothing is to be told that— There again we lack a definition, do we not? Never mind. We shall understand. You knew her in Germany?"

"Yes."

"And she—You wear a mask, at moments even merry-faced, but now and again I have surprised a look of such sadness in your eyes that—Is that why you came to America? She"—

"No. She was, and is, in so different a class, that I never"—

"You should not allow that to be a bar! Any woman"—

"But even more, there are other claims upon me, which make marriage out of the question."

"And this is why you have resigned reputation for money-making? Is there no escape? Oh, it seems too cruel to be!"

"You draw it worse than it is, Miss Walton, forgetting that I told you of my happiness in loving."

"You make me proud to feel that we are friends, Dr. Hartzmann," you said gently. "I hope she is worthy of such a love?"

I merely nodded; and after a slight pause you remarked, "Now it is only fair to give you a turn." I had been pondering, after my first impulsive assent, over my right to win your confidence, with the one inevitable conclusion that was so clear, and I answered, "I have no questions to ask, Miss Walton."

"Then I can ask no more, of course," you replied quietly, and at once turned the conversation into less personal subjects, until the time came for our return to My Fancy. When we parted in the upper hall, that evening, you said to me, "I always value your opinion, and it usually influences me. Do you, as your speech to-night implied, think it right to go on loving baseness?"

"It is not a question of right and wrong, but only whether the love remains." "Then you don't think it a duty to crush it out?"

"No. All love is noble that is distinct from self."

You held out your hand. "I am so glad you think so, and that you spoke your thought. You have done me a great kindness,—greater far than you can ever know. Thank you, and good-night."

Good-night, Maizie.

XX

March 11. When I left My Fancy, after my visit, Agnes had nothing but praise for me. "I was certain that you and Maizie would be friends if you ever really knew each other," she said triumphantly. Unfortunately, our first meeting in the city served only to prove the reverse. In one of my daily walks up-town, I met you and Agnes outside a shop where you had been buying Christmas gifts for the boys of your Neighborhood Guild. You were looking for the carriage, about which there had been some mistake, and I helped you search. When our hunt was unsuccessful, you both said you would rather walk than let me get a cab, having been deterred only by the growing darkness, and not by the snow. So chatting merrily, away we went, through the elfin flakes which seemed so eager to kiss your cheeks, till your home was reached.

"If we come in, will you give us some tea?" asked Agnes.

"Tea, cake, chocolates, and conversation," you promised.

"I am sorry," I said, "but I cannot spare the time."

I thought you and Agnes exchanged glances. "Please, Doc—" she began; but you interrupted her by saying proudly, "We must not take any more of Dr. Hartzmann's time, Agnes. Will you come in?"

"No," replied Agnes. "I'll go home before it's any darker. Good-night."

I started to walk with her the short distance, but the moment we were out of hearing she turned towards me and cried, "I hate you!" As I made no reply, she demanded impatiently, "What makes you behave so abominably?" When I was still silent she continued: "I told you how Maizie felt, and I thought it was all right, and now you do it again. It's too bad! Well, can't you say something? Why do you do it?"

"There is nothing for me to say, Miss Blodgett," I responded sadly.

"You might at least do it to please me," she persisted, "even if you don't like Maizie."

I made no answer, and we walked the rest of the distance in silence. At the stoop, however, Agnes asked, "Will you go with me to call on Maizie, some afternoon?"

I shook my head.

"Not even to please mamma and me?" she questioned.

Again I gave the same answer, and without a word of parting she left me and passed through the doorway. From that time she has treated me coldly.

Another complication only tended to increase the coldness, as well as to involve me with Mrs. Blodgett. In December, Mr. Blodgett came into Mr. Whitely's office and announced, "I've been taking a liberty with your name, doctor."

"For what kindness am I indebted now?" I inquired.

"I'm a member of the Philomathean," he said,—"not because I'm an author, or artist, or engineer, or scientist, but because I'm a big frog in my own puddle, and they want samples of us, provided we are good fellows, just to see what we're like. I was talking with Professor Eaton in September, and we agreed you ought to be one of us; so we stuck your name up, and Saturday evening the club elected you."

"I can't afford it"—I began; but he interrupted with:—

"I knew you'd say that, and so didn't tell you beforehand. I'll bet you your initiation fee and a year's dues against a share of R. T. common that you'll make enough out of your membership to pay you five times over."

"How can I do that?"

"All the editors and publishers are members," he replied, "and to meet them over the rum punch we serve on meeting nights is worth money to the most celebrated author living. Then you'll have the best club library in this country at your elbow for working purposes."

"I don't think I ought, Mr. Blodgett."

He was about to protest, when Mr. Whitely broke in upon us, saying, "Accept your membership, Dr. Hartzmann, and the paper shall pay your initiation and dues."

I do not know whether Mr. Blodgett or myself was the more surprised at this unexpected and liberal offer. Our amazement was so obvious that Mr. Whitely continued: "I think it'll be an excellent idea for the paper to have a member of its staff in the Philomathean, and so the office shall pay for it."

"Whitely," observed Mr. Blodgett admiringly, "you're a good business man, whatever else you are!"

"I wish, Blodgett," inquired Mr. Whitely, "you would tell me why I have been kept waiting so long?"

"Many a name's been up longer than yours," replied Mr. Blodgett in a comforting voice. "You don't seem to realize that the Philomathean's a pretty stiff club to get into."

"But I've been posted for over three years, while here Dr. Hartzmann is elected within four months of his proposing."

"Well, the doctor has the great advantage of being a sort of natural Philomath, you see," Mr. Blodgett explained genially. "He was born that way, and so is ripe for membership without any closet mellowing."

"But my reputation as a writer is greater than Dr."—began Mr. Whitely; but a laugh from Mr. Blodgett made him halt.

"Oh come, now, Whitely!"

"What's the matter?" asked my employer.

"Once St. Peter and St. Paul stopped at a tavern to quench their thirst," said Mr. Blodgett, "and when the time came to pay, they tossed dice for it. Paul threw double sixes, and smiled. Peter smiled back, and threw double sevens. What do you suppose Paul said, Whitely?"

"What?"

"'Oh, Peter, Peter! No miracles between friends.'"

"I don't follow you," rejoined Mr. Whitely.

Mr. Blodgett turned and said to me, "I'm going West for two months, and while I'm gone the Twelfth-night revel at the Philomathean is to come off. Will you see that the boss and Agnes get cards?" Then he faced about and remarked, "Whitely, I'd give a big gold certificate to know what nerve food you use!" and went out, laughing.

When I took the invitations to Mrs. Blodgett, I found you all with your heads full of a benefit for the Guild, to be given at your home,—a musical evening, with several well-known stars as magnets, and admission by invitation as an additional attraction. Mrs. Blodgett said to me in her decisive way, "Dr. Hartzmann, the invitations are five dollars each, and you are to take one."

I half suspected that it was only a device to get me within your doors, though every society woman feels at liberty to whitemail her social circle to an unlimited degree. But the fact that the entertainment was to be in your home, even more than my poverty, compelled me to refuse to be a victim of her charitable kindness or her charitable greed. I merely shook my head.

"Oh, but you must," she urged. "It will be a delightful evening, and then it's such a fine object."

"Do not ask it of Dr. Hartzmann," you protested, coming to my aid. "No one"—

"I'm sure it's very little to ask," remarked Mrs. Blodgett, in a disappointed way.

"Mrs. Blodgett," I said, in desperation, "for years I have denied myself every luxury and almost every comfort. I have lived at the cheapest of boarding-houses; I have walked down-town, rain or shine, to save ten cents a day; I have"—I stopped there, ashamed of my outbreak.

"I suppose, Dr. Hartzmann," retorted Agnes, with no attempt to conceal the irritation she felt toward me, "that the Philomathean is one of your ten-cent economies?"

Before I could speak you changed the subject, and the matter was dropped,—I hoped for all time. It was, however, to reappear, and to make my position more difficult and painful than ever.

At Mrs. Blodgett's request, made that very day, I sent you an invitation to the Philomathean ladies' day. It was with no hope of being there myself, since my editorial duties covered the hours of the exhibition; but good or bad fortune aided me, for Mr. Whitely asked me for a ticket, and his absence from the office set me free. The crowd was great, but, like most people who try for one thing only, I attained my desire by quickly finding you, and we spent an enjoyable hour together, studying the delicious jokes and pranks of our artist members. The truly marvelous admixture of absurdity and cleverness called out the real mirth of your nature, and our happiness and gayety over the pictures strangely recalled to me our similar days spent in Paris and elsewhere. You too, I think, remembered the same experience, for when we had finished, and were ascending the stairs to the dining-room, you remarked to me, "I never dreamed that one could be so merry after one had ceased to be a child. For the last hour I have felt as if teens were yet unventured lands."

I confess I sought a secluded spot in an alcove, hoping still to keep you to myself; but the project failed, for when I returned from getting you an ice, I found that Mr. Whitely had joined you. The pictures, of course, were the subject of discussion, and you asked him, "Are all the other members as clever in their own professions as your artists have shown themselves to be?"

"The Philomathean is made up of an able body of men," replied Mr. Whitely in a delightfully patronizing tone. "Some few of the very ablest, perhaps, do not care to be members; but of the second rank, you may say, broadly speaking, that it includes all men of prominence in this city."

"But why should the abler men not belong?"

"They are too occupied with more vital matters," explained my employer.

"Yet surely they must need a club, and what one so appropriate as this?"

"It is natural to reason so," assented the would-be member. "But as an actual fact, some of the most prominent men in this city are not members," and he mentioned three well-known names.

The inference was so unjust that I observed, "Should you not add, Mr. Whitely, that they are not members either because they know it is useless to apply, or because they have applied in vain; and that their exclusion, though superficially a small affair, probably means to them, by the implication it carries, one of the keenest mortifications of their lives?"

"You mean that the Philomathean refuses to admit such men as Mr. Whitely named?" you asked incredulously.

I smiled. "The worldly reputation and the professional reputation of men occasionally differ very greatly, Miss Walton. We do not accept a man here because his name appears often in the newspapers, but because of what the men of his own calling know and think of him."

"And of course they are always jealous of a man who has surpassed them," contended Mr. Whitely.

"There must be something more against a man than envy of his confrères to exclude him," I answered. "My loyalty to the Philomathean, Miss Walton, is due to the influence it exerts in this very matter. Errors are possible, but the intention is that no man shall be of our brotherhood who is not honestly doing something worth the doing, for other reasons than mere money-making. And for that very reason, we are supposed, within these walls, to be friends, whether or not there is acquaintance outside of them. We are the one club in New York which dares to trust its membership list implicitly to that extent. Charlatanry and dishonesty may succeed with the world, but here they fail. Money will buy much, but the poorest man stands on a par here with the wealthiest."

"You make me envious of you both," you sighed, just as Mrs. Blodgett and Agnes joined us.

"What are you envying them?" asked Agnes, as she shook hands with you,—"that they were monopolizing you? How selfish men are!"

"In monopolizing this club?"

"Was that what you envied them?" ejaculated Mrs. Blodgett. "I for one am glad there's a place to which I can't go, where I can send my husband when

I want to be rid of him." Then she turned to Mr. Whitely, and with her usual directness remarked, "So they've let you in? Mr. Blodgett told me you would surely be rejected."

Mr. Whitely reddened and bit his lip, for which he is hardly to be blamed. But he only bowed slightly in reply, leaving the inference in your minds that he was a Philomath. How the man dares so often to—

The striking clock tells me it is later than I thought, and I must stop.

Good-night, dear heart.

XXI

March 12. Our talk at the Philomathean and Mr. Whitely's tacit assumption of membership had their penalty for me,—a penalty which, to reverse the old adage, I first thought an undisguised blessing. When we separated, he asked me to dinner the following evening, to fill in a place unexpectedly left vacant; and as I knew, from a chance allusion, that you were to be there, I accepted a courtesy at his hands.

Although there were several celebrities at the meal, it fell to my lot to sit on your right; my host, who took you down, evidently preferring to have no dangerous rival in your attention. But Mrs. Blodgett, who sat on his other side, engaged him as much as she chose, and thus gave me more of your time than I should otherwise have had. If you knew how happy it made me that, whenever she interrupted his monopoly of you, instead of making a trialogue with them, you never failed to turn to me!

"I have just re-read Mr. Whitely's book," you remarked, in one of these interruptions, "and I have been trying to express to him my genuine admiration for it. I thought of it highly when first I read it, last autumn, but on a second reading I have become really an enthusiast."

I suppose my face must have shown some of the joy your words gave me, for you continued, "Clearly, you like it too, and are pleased to hear it praised. But then it's notorious that writers are jealous of one another! Tell me what you think of it?"

I tried to keep all bitterness out of my voice as I laughed. "Think how unprofessional it would be in me to discuss my employer's book: if I praised it, how necessary; if I disparaged it, how disloyal!"

"You are as unsatisfactory as Mr. Whitely," you complained. "I can't get him to speak about it, either. He smiles and bows his head to my praise, but not a word can he be made to say. Evidently he has a form of modesty—not stage fright, but book fright—that I never before encountered. Every other author I have met was fatiguingly anxious to talk about his own writings."

"Remember in our behalf that a book stands very much in the same relation to a writer that a baby does to its mother. We are tolerant of her admiration; be equally lenient to the author's harmless prattle."

"I suppose, too," you went on, "that the historian is less liable to the disease, because his work is so much less his own flesh and blood; so much less emotional than that of the poet or novelist."

"No book worth reading ever fails to be steeped with the spirit of the person who wrote it. The man on the stage is instinct with emotion and feeling, but does he express more of his true individuality than the man in real life? The historian puts fewer of his own feelings into his work, but he plays far less to the gallery, and so is more truthful in what he reveals of himself."

"Your simile reminds me of a thought of my own, after my first reading of this book: that the novelist is the demagogue of letters, striving to please, and suing for public favor by catering to all its whims and weaknesses; but the historian is the aristocrat of literature, knowing the right, and proudly above taking heed of popular prejudice or moods. I liked Mr. Whitely's book for many things, but most of all for its fearless attitude towards whatever it touched upon. I felt that it was the truth, because the whole atmosphere told me that a man was writing, too brave to tell what was untrue. That evidently pleases you, again," you laughed. "Oh, it is horrible to see this consuming jealousy!"

When the ladies withdrew, the men, as usual, clustered at one end of the table; but my host beckoned me to join him, and sat down apart from his guests.

"Dr. Hartzmann, what is the matter at the Philomathean?" he demanded, in a low voice.

"Matter?" I questioned.

"Yes. What is the reason they don't elect me?"

"I am not on the membership committee, Mr. Whitely," I replied.

"Are you popular up there? Mr. Blodgett said that you were."

"I have some good friends," I answered.

"Then electioneer and get me put in," he explained, revealing to me in a flash why he had volunteered that the paper should pay the expenses of my membership.

"I am hardly in a position to do that."

"Why not?"

"I am a new member, and my position under you is so well known that it would be very indelicate in me to appear in the matter."

"For what do you suppose I helped you, then?" he asked severely.

"I did not understand till now."

"Well, then, drop your talk about delicacy, and get your friends to elect me."

"I do not think I can do that," I answered mildly.

"Then you won't earn your pay?"

"Mr. Whitely, when you made the offer, you put it on an entirely different ground, and it is unfair to claim that it involved any condition that was not then expressed."

"But you ought to be willing to do it. Haven't you any gratitude about you?"

"I understood that you wanted one of your staff a member of that club. Had you mentioned your present motive, I should certainly have refused to accept the offer; and under these circumstances I decline to recognize any cause for gratitude."

"What is your objection to doing it, though?" he persisted.

"Indeed, Mr. Whitely, I do not think I am called upon to say more than I have said."

"Do you want me in the club or not?" he demanded.

"I shall certainly never oppose your election in any way whatsoever."

"But you will not work for me?"

"No."

"Are you waiting to see how much I'll give?"

My hand trembled at the insult, but I made no reply.

"Come," he continued, "are you standing out in hopes I will offer you something?"

"No."

"How much?" he asked.

"I have been elected to the Philomathean, Mr. Whitely," I said, concluding that an explanation might be the easiest escape, after all, "and to it I owe a distinct duty. If you were not my employer, I should feel called upon to work against you."

"Why?" he exclaimed, in surprise.

"Is it necessary to say?" I answered.

"Yes. What is your objection to me?"

"Did you never read Æsop's fable of the jackdaw?" I asked.

"That's it, is it? And you are opposing my election?"

"By not the slightest act."

"Then why did Blodgett predict that I would surely be rejected? I've a reputation as a writer, as a philanthropist, and as a successful business man. What more do they want?"

"As I told Miss Walton yesterday," I explained, "a man's true and eventual reputation depends, not on what the world thinks of him, but on what his fellow-craft decide."

"Well?"

"There is scarcely an author or editor at the Philomathean who is not opposed to your election, Mr. Whitely."

"You have been telling tales," he muttered angrily.

"You should know better."

"Then what have they against me?"

"Any man who works with his pen learns that no one can write either editorials or books, of the kind credited to you, without years of training. The most embarrassing ordeal I have to undergo is the joking and questioning with which the fraternity tease me. But you need never fear my not keeping faith."

"Yet you won't help me into the Philomathean?"

"No."

"So you'll make money out of me, but think your club too good?"

"I owe my club a duty."

"I know," he went on smoothly, "that you're an awful screw, when there's a dollar in sight. How much do you want?"

My silence should have warned him, but he was too self-absorbed to feel anything but his own mood.

"How much do you want?" he repeated, and I still sat without speaking, though the room blurred, and I felt as if I were stifling. "The day I'm elected to the Philomathean, I'll give you"—

I rose and interrupted him, saying, "Mr. Whitely, if you wish me to leave your house and employment, you can obtain my absence in an easier way than by insulting me."

For a moment we faced each other in silence, and then he rose. "Hereafter, Dr. Hartzmann, you will pay those dues yourself," he said in a low voice, as he moved towards the door.

I only bowed, glad that the matter was so easily ended; and for nearly two months our relations have been of the most formal kind that can exist between employer and employed.

Far more bitter was another break. When the moment of farewell came, that evening, I waited to put you and Mrs. Blodgett into your carriages, and while we were delayed in the vestibule you thanked me again for the pleasure of the previous afternoon, and then continued: "I understand why you did not feel able to please Mrs. Blodgett about the concert. But won't you let me acknowledge the pleasure of yesterday by sending you a ticket? I have taken a number, and as all my circle have done the same, I am finding it rather difficult to get rid of them."

"That's all right, Maizie," interjected Mrs. Blodgett, who had caught, or inferred from an occasional word that she heard, what you were saying. "We took an extra ticket, and I am going to use the doctor for an escort that evening."

"I thank you both," I answered, "but I shall not be able to attend the concert."

"Nonsense!" sniffed Mrs. Blodgett, as I helped her into her carriage. "You're going to do as I tell you."

You did not speak in the moment we waited for your coupé to take its place, but as the tiger opened the door you looked in my face for the first time since my words, showing me eyes that told of the pain I had inflicted.

"I am sorry," you said quietly. "I had thought—hoped—that we were to be friends."

There was nothing for me to say, and we parted thus. From that time I have seen little of you, for when I meet you now you no longer make it possible for me to have much of your society. And my persistent refusal to go to the concert with Mrs. Blodgett and Agnes increased their irritation against me, so that I am no longer asked to their home, and thus have lost my most frequent opportunity of meeting you. But harder even than this deprivation is the thought that I have given you pain; made all the greater, perhaps, because so ill deserved and apparently unreasonable. I find myself longing for the hour when we shall meet at that far-away tribunal, where all our lives, and not alone that which is seen, will stand revealed. For two months I have not had a single moment of happiness or even hope. I am lonely and weary, while my strength and courage seem to lessen day by day. Oh, my darling, I pray God that thought of you will make me stronger and braver, that I may go on with my fight. Good-night.

XXII

March 13. Last night, at the Philomathean, Mr. Blodgett joined me, and asked me why I had not dined with them lately. He returned only a few days ago, and was thus ignorant that I have not been inside his door for weeks. I hesitated for an instant, and then replied, "I have been working very hard."

"What are you usually doing?" he asked, smiling. "Come in to Sunday dinner to-morrow."

"I shall be too busy with a lot of manuscripts I have on hand, that must be read," I told him.

"Stop killing yourself," he ordered. "As it is, you look as if you were on the brink of a bad illness. You won't get on a bit faster by dying young."

There the matter rested, and I did not go to dinner to-day, being indeed glad to stay indoors; for I very foolishly walked up town yesterday through the slush, and caught a bad cold. While I was trying to keep warm, this evening, a note was brought me from Mr. Blodgett, asking me to come to him at once; and fearing something important, I braved the cold without delay, ill though I felt. I was shown at once into his den, which was so cheerful with its open fire that I felt it was a good exchange for my cold room, where I had sat coughing and shivering all the afternoon.

"Twice in my life I've really lost my temper with the boss," he began, before I had even sat down, though he closed the door while speaking. "Never mind about the first time, but to-day I got mad enough to last me for the rest of my life."

"May I sit down?" I interrupted.

He nodded his head, and took a position in front of me, with his back to the fire, as he continued: "Women are enough to make a man frantic when they get a fixed idea! Now, to-day, at dinner, I said I'd invited you, and I saw in a moment something was in the wind; so when we had finished I told them to come in here, and it didn't take me long to find out the trouble."

"I didn't like to"—I began; but he went on:—

"And that was the beginning of their trouble. I tell you, there was Cain here for about ten minutes, and there weren't two worse scared women this side of the grave, while I was ranting; for the boss remembered the other time, and Agnes had never seen me break loose. I told them they'd done their best to drive you crazy with grief; that if they'd searched for ten years they couldn't have found a meaner or crueler thing, or one that would have hurt you more; that nine men out of ten, in your shoes, would have acted dishonestly or cut their throat, but that you had toed the chalk-line right along, and never once winced. And I let them know that for five dollars they'd added the last straw of pain to a fellow who deserved only kindness and help from them."

"Really, Mr. Blodgett"—I protested.

"Hold on. Don't attempt to stop me, for the fit's on me still," he growled. "They tried to come the surprised, and then the offended, but they didn't fool me. I never let up on them till I had said all I wanted to say, and they won't forget it for a day or two. When I sent Agnes upstairs, she was sobbing her eyes out, and the boss would have given her pin money for ten years to have escaped with her."

"It's too bad to"—

"That's just what it was!" he cried. "To think of those screws trying to blackmail you, and then telling me you were a skinflint because you wouldn't do what they wanted! Well, after Agnes had gone, I gave the boss a supplementary and special dose of her own. I told her she could double discount you on meanness, and then give you forty-nine points; and to make sure of good measurement, I added in the whole female sex along with her. I told her that if she knew the facts of your life, she'd get down on her knees and crawl round to your place to ask your pardon, and then she wouldn't be fit to have it. I told her that when the day of judgment came, she'd just go the other way in preference to hearing what the recording angel had written of her."

"I am afraid that your intended kindness will make my welcome scantier than ever."

"Not a bit of it. I'm the master of this house, as they found out this afternoon, and I say who'll come into it, and who'll not. I shan't need to interfere in your case, for you'll get a warm welcome from both."

"You didn't tell them?" I exclaimed, starting forward in my seat.

"Not a word, though the boss nearly went crazy with curiosity. But I did say that you were making a splendid up-hill fight, and if they knew the facts of the case they'd be proud to black your boots. My word goes in this family about as well as it does on the Street, and you'll get all the welcome you can stand from now on."

"You make me very proud and happy."

"You have reason to be proud," he asserted. "I'm not a man who slobbers much, but I'm going to tell you what I think of you. When you first came here, I sized you up as rather a softy, your manner was so quiet and gentle. I got over that delusion precious quick, and I want to say that for pluck and grit you're a trump, and there's my hand on it."

He went to the table, poured out a couple of glasses of whiskey and seltzer, and brought them to the fire. "You need something for that graveyard cough of yours," he said, handing one to me. "Well," he went on, "I didn't bring you out such a night as this to tell you of my scrap; but after the row, the boss was so ashamed of herself that she trumped up an A 1 excuse (as she thought) for having treated you as she had, and that led to a talk, and that's why I sent round for you. What do you suppose she has got into her head?"

"I can't imagine."

"I needn't tell you," he remarked, "that women always know an awful lot that isn't so. But just because they do, they every now and then discover a truth that can't be come at in any other way. Now the boss thinks she's done this, and I'm not sure that she hasn't. She says you are in love."

"I never knew a man who wasn't," I replied, trying to smile. "If it isn't with a woman, then it's always with himself."

"But the boss thinks she knows the girl, and has a down on you because you—because you don't try for her."

I laughed bitterly, and said, "You needed no explanation for that."

"That's what made the boss's idea reasonable to me," he explained. "She couldn't conceive why you should keep silent, and so was ready to pitch into you on the slightest pretense. Women haven't much use for a man who falls in love and doesn't say so. But of course I knew that your debt put marriage out of the question."

I merely nodded my head, for even to him I could not speak of my love for you, it was so sacred to me.

He drew up a chair to the fire, and continued: "There isn't another man to whom I'd care to say what I'm going to say to you, but you've got a heart and a head both, and won't misunderstand me." He finished his glass, and set it on the mantel. "Now I don't have to tell you that the boss is fond of you, and when I told her that I knew of a reason why you couldn't marry, she forgave you on the spot. What's more, she first wished to learn what it was; and failing in that, she then wanted to know if it could be remedied, so that you might have a chance to win the girl."

"She of course knows nothing of my position?"

"No," he said, "but she knows something of your character, and she's ordered me that, if it's possible, I'm to help you get the girl you care for."

"But my debt!" I exclaimed.

"How much is it now?" he queried.

"One hundred and eighteen thousand."

"Well, I'll lend Agnes's husband one hundred and eighteen thousand dollars at three per cent, and leave her the note when I die. From what I know of marriage, I venture to assert that if she squeezes him for payment it will be his own fault."

I sat speechless for a moment, too bewildered by the unexpected turn to even think.

"I was as surprised as you look," he went on, "for although I had seen that you and Agnes"—

"Indeed, Mr. Blodgett," I exclaimed hastily, "I am no more to Miss Agnes than a dozen of her friends! I"—

"So the boss says," he interrupted. "But that doesn't mean that you can't be. Though to speak the truth, my boy," he continued, resting his hand on my knee, "this wasn't my plan. I had hoped that you and Maizie would take a shine to each other, and so kiss the chalk-marks off that old score. But when I spoke of the scheme to the boss, this evening, she told me there had never been a chance of it; that you didn't like Mai, and that she is practically engaged to Whitely, and is only—Better have some more whiskey, or that cough will shake you to pieces."

I could only shake my head in my misery, but after a moment I was able to say, "Mr. Blodgett, I did not understand—I"—

"I want to tell you," he broke in, "before you say anything more, that I never believe in putting one's fingers into love affairs, and I shouldn't in this case if the boss didn't feel so keen about it, but I don't choose to be the one to stand in her way. And now I'm not offering my daughter's hand. You know as well as I that Agnes isn't the kind of girl who needs a prospectus or a gold clause to work her off. If she dropped her handkerchief to-morrow, fifty men would be scrambling for it, eh?"

"Yes." Then I added, "And, Mr. Blodgett, I can't find the words to tell how I thank you both for such a compliment. If"—

"I knew you wouldn't misunderstand me," he went on. "It's a good deal of a start in life to be born a gentleman."

"But, Mr. Blodgett," I said, "there has been a mistake. I—it is hard to say, but"—then I faltered.

He looked at me keenly for a moment. "So the boss was wrong? It's only friendship, not love?"

"Just what she has given to me," I answered.

"Very well. Then if you want to please the boss—and me—let that friendship grow into something better. But don't misunderstand me. You must win Agnes, if she is won. We do nothing."

"Mr. Blodgett, should you be willing to let me try to win Miss Agnes, if I tell you that I do not love her as a man should love the woman he seeks for his wife?"

"Marriage is a funny business," he responded. "Now there's the boss. When I married her I thought she was so and so; little by little I found she wasn't; but by the time I had found it out I wouldn't have swapped her for ten of the women I had thought she was. Some men have no business to marry unless they're pretty strongly attached, for they don't run steady; but you're a fellow that would keep in the traces no matter what happened, and before long you'd find yourself mighty fond of Agnes. A sense of duty is about as good a basis to marry on, if there's natural sympathy and liking, as all this ideal make-believe. I don't think you dislike Agnes, do you?"

"Indeed, no!" I exclaimed. "Nobody could. She is too charming and sweet for any one to do that. Miss Agnes deserves far more than I can bring her. What have I to give in return for all this?"

"You can settle that with Agnes," he laughed; and then, as if to lessen my poverty in my own eyes, he kindly added, "In the first place, I'll get a son-in-law chock-full of heart and grit and brains; and I've had pretty good evidence that he isn't fortune-hunting, which is Agnes's great danger. But that isn't all, and I want you to know I'm not a fool. I'm a big fellow down in Wall Street, and even on the Royal Exchange, but do you think I don't know my position? They kept me up over two years at the Philomathean, and you four months. After you've worked ten years over books with your own name on them, you'll be received and kotowed to by people who wouldn't crook a finger to know me. You won't be famous as I am, for the number of naughts I can write after a figure, but your name will be known everywhere, and will be familiar long after mine has been forgotten. Who were the bankers and rich men fifty years ago? There isn't one person in a thousand can tell you. But who hasn't heard of Thackeray and Hawthorne,

Macaulay and Motley? My girl will have more money than she'll need; so if she gets a good husband, and one with reputation, she can't do better. Don't you see I'm doing my level best for Agnes, and making a regular Jew bargain?"

"Perhaps Miss Agnes will not agree."

"We've got to take that chance; but she likes you, and good women think a heap more of brains than they do of money. If you'll let me tell her your story, it won't be long before she'll take notice. I shouldn't have had to ask the boss twice if I'd had any such trump card as you've got, and she was a sight less tender-hearted than Agnes!"

"Mr. Blodgett," I said, "I can't tell you the gratitude I feel, but I must be frank."

"Hold on!" he cried. "I don't want you to say anything now. You are to take a week on it, and not give me your answer till the end. If you have half the gratitude in you that you pretend, you'll do as the boss wants."

I had manned myself to tell him of my love for you, but I bowed assent, for indeed, I was too bewildered to think clearly, and was glad to have a respite. We shook hands without further parley, and I came back here, to cough and shiver while trying to think it all out. An hour ago I went to bed, but I was wakeful, and so sit here trying to write myself into sleepiness.

I have thought out what my course must be. If it is true, as indeed I know it to be, that Mr. Whitely has won you, Mr. Blodgett shall have the truth. I shall tell him that I will put you out of my heart, as perforce I must, and that if he is still willing I will go to Agnes, tell her too the whole truth, and promise her such love and devotion as I can give. So sweet a girl deserves far more, and I cannot believe that she will accept the little I can offer; but if she does, it shall be the labor of my life to be to her a true and tender husband. And even if she were not what she is, the thought that through her I have made reparation for the wrong done you will make easy both tenderness and love for her.

For the last time, perhaps, I have the right to say, "Good-night, my love."

XXIII

March 14. After dinner this evening I went to see Mrs. Blodgett; for, miserable as I felt, my mental suffering was greater than my physical. The footman told me she had just gone upstairs to dress for a ball, but I sent her a message begging for a moment's interview; and when he returned, it was to take me to her boudoir,—a privilege which would in itself have shown me how thoroughly I was forgiven, even if her greeting had been less warm.

In a few halting and broken sentences I told her of my love for you. She was so amazed that at first she seemed unable to believe me serious; and when I had persuaded her that I was in earnest, her perplexity and curiosity were unbounded.

Why had I behaved so? For what reason had I never called on Maizie? Such and many more were the questions she indignantly poured out, and she only grew more angry when I answered each by "I cannot tell you." Finally, in her irritation, she demanded, "What have you bothered me for, then?"

"I want you to tell me, if you have the right, whether Miss Walton is engaged to Mr. Whitely," I answered.

"Practically," she snapped.

"She has told you so?"

"I cannot tell you," she replied; adding, "How do you like your own medicine?"

"Mrs. Blodgett," I pleaded, "if you understood what it means to me to know the truth, you would not use this to punish me for what I cannot help. If I could tell any one the story of my life, I should tell you; for next to—to one other, you are dearer to me than any living person. If you love me at all, do not torture me with a suspense that is unbearable."

She came and sat down by me on the lounge, and took my hand, saying, "Mr. Whitely asked Maizie to marry him four years ago, but she said she would not marry a business man. He wouldn't give up trying, however, though he made no apparent headway. Indeed, Maizie told me herself, last spring, just before she sailed, that she could never love him, and she was convinced that loveless marriages were wrong, being sure to end in unhappiness or sacrifice of one or the other. So I thought it would come to nothing. But he persisted, and he's succeeded, for she told me last week that she had changed her mind, and was going to marry him."

"Do you know why she has done so?" I asked drearily.

"I think it is that book of his. Not merely is she pleased by the position it's given him as a writer, but she says it has convinced her that he is different from what he appears in society; that no man but one of noble character and fine mind could write from such a standpoint."

I sat there dumb and stolid, yet knowing that all my past suffering had been as nothing to this new grief. Oh, my blindness and wickedness! To think, my darling, that it was I who had aided him to win you, that my hand had made and set the trap! Why had I not ended my wretched existence three years ago, and so, at least, saved myself from this second wrong, tenfold worse than that I had endeavored to mend? For my own selfish pride and honor, I had juggled, deceived you, Maizie, the woman dearer to me than all else, and had myself doomed you to such a fate.

I suppose I must have shown some of the agony I felt, for Mrs. Blodgett put her hand on my shoulder. "Don't take it so to heart, Rudolph," she begged, giving me that name for the first time. "There can still be much true happiness in your life."

I only kissed her hand in response, but she instantly pressed her lips on my forehead. "I am so sorry," she sighed, "for I had hoped for something very different."

"Mr. Blodgett told me," I answered; and then I spoke of the resolution I had come to last night.

When I had finished, she said, "We won't talk of it any more, Rudolph, for Agnes' sake as well as yours, but perhaps by and by, when the suffering is over, you will come and talk to me again; for if you ever feel that you can be a good husband to my girl, I shall not be afraid to trust her to you, if you can gain her consent."

I rose to go, and she remarked, "Yes. You mustn't stay, for as it is, my dressing will make us very late. If the carriage is at the door, tell Maxwell to drive you home, and then return for us. You mustn't walk in the slush with that horrid cough of yours. Does your landlady give you blankets enough? Well, tell her to make a steaming glass of whiskey toddy. Wrap some woolen round your throat and chest, and go straight to bed. Why, Rudolph, you are not going without kissing me good-night?" she continued, as if that had been my habit, adding, "Some day I shall make you tell me all about it."

I went downstairs, intending to follow her directions; but as I passed the drawing-room door I heard the piano, and thought I recognized, from the touch, whose fingers were straying at random over the keys.

"Isn't that Miss Walton?" I asked of the servant, as he brought me my hat and coat.

"Yes, Dr. Hartzmann. Miss Walton is to go to the ball with the ladies, and is waiting for them to come downstairs," he told me.

I left him holding my coat, and passed noiselessly between the curtains of the portière. Your back was turned to me as you sat at the instrument, and I stood in silence watching you as you played, till suddenly—was it sympathy, or only the consciousness of something alien?—you looked around. I should almost think it was the former, for you expressed no surprise at seeing me standing there, even though you rose.

"Don't let me interrupt you," I begged.

"I was only beguiling the time I have to wait," you replied.

"It will be a favor to me if you will go on," I said, and without another word, with that simple grace and sweetness natural to you, you resumed your seat and went on playing, while I sat down on the divan.

Your bent, like mine, was for some reason a sad one, and what you played reflected your mood, stirring me deeply and making me almost forget my misery. Presently, however, I was seized with a paroxysm of coughing; and when I had recovered enough to be conscious of anything, I found you standing by me, looking both startled and compassionate.

"You are ill, Dr. Hartzmann," you said, anxiously.

"It is nothing," I managed to articulate.

"Can I do anything for you?" you asked.

"Nothing," I replied, rising, more wretched than ever, because knowing how little I deserved your sympathy.

"It would be a pleasure to help you, Dr. Hartzmann, for I have never been able to show any gratefulness for your kindness over my book," you went on, with a touch of timidity in your tones, as if you were asking a favor rather than conferring one.

Won by your manner, before I knew what I was doing, I spoke. "Miss Walton," I burst out, "you see before you the most miserable being conceivable, and you can save me from the worst anguish I am suffering!"

Your eyes enlarged in surprise, both at my vehemence and at what I had uttered, while you stood looking at me, with slightly parted lips; then you said sweetly, "Tell me what I can do for you."

I had spoken without thought, only conscious that I must try in some way to save you. For a moment I hesitated, and then exclaimed, "I beg of you not to marry Mr. Whitely!"

Like a goddess you drew yourself up, even before you could have appreciated the full import of my foolish speech, and never have I seen you look more beautiful or queenly than as you faced me. After a brief silence you answered, "You can hardly realize what you are saying, Dr. Hartzmann."

"I am indeed mad in my unhappiness," I groaned.

"You owe me an explanation for your extraordinary words," you continued.

"Miss Walton," I said, "Mr. Whitely is not a man to make you happy, and in hopes of saving you from him I spoke as I did. I had no right, as none can know better than myself, but perhaps you will forgive the impertinence when I say that my motive was only to save you from future misery."

"Why should I not be happy in marrying Mr. Whitely?"

"Because you are deceiving yourself about him."

"In what respect?"

"His character is other than you think it."

"Be more specific."

"That I cannot be."

"Why not?"

"It would be dishonorable in me."

"Not more so than to stop where you have."

"I cannot say more."

"I do not recognize your right to be silent. You have said too much or too little."

"Maizie," called Mrs. Blodgett from the hall, "come quickly, for we are very late."

"I shall insist, at some future time, upon your speaking more clearly, Dr. Hartzmann," you said, as a queen would speak, and picking up your wrap, without a parting word, you left me standing in the middle of the drawing-room.

I came home through the cold, and have sat here regretting my foolishness and groping for the right course to pursue. Oh, my darling, if I but had the right, I would gladly tell you the whole story of the miserable deception, even though I disgraced myself in your eyes. If it were merely my own honor which was at stake, I should not hesitate for an instant, but would sacrifice it to save you, though self-respect seems now the only thing left me. But try as I may to prove to myself that I have the right, I cannot, for I feel that more than my own honor is concerned. I have taken Mr. Whitely's money, and cannot return it to him. To break faith would be worse than despicable. I shall speak to you of my employer's hardness, and beg you to ask Mr. Blodgett if he would give Agnes to Mr. Whitely or advise you to marry him. My heart yearns to aid you in your peril, but I can think of nothing more that I can do. May God do what I cannot, my dearest. Good-night.

XXIV

March 15. I was so miserable with my cough to-day that I could not summon the energy to drag myself to Mr. Blodgett's office, and did not leave my room till after eight, when your note came.

"Miss Walton," it read, "feels that she has the right to request Dr. Hartzmann to call this evening, in relation to the conversation uncompleted last night."

I understood the implied command, and thought that I owed what you claimed, while feeling that in obeying I could for this once forego my scruple of entering your door. The footman showed me into the library, and left me there. It was the first time I had seen it since my thirteenth year, and I cannot tell you the moment's surprise and joy I felt on finding it absolutely unchanged. Even the books were arranged as formerly, and my eye searched and found, as quickly as of yore, all the old volumes full of plates which had once given us such horror and delight. For the instant I forgot my physical suffering and the coming ordeal.

When you entered the room, you welcomed me only with a bow. Then seeing my paleness, you said kindly, "I forgot your cough, Dr. Hartzmann, or I would not have brought you out in such weather. Sit here by the fire." After a short pause you went on: "I hope that a day's thought has convinced you that common justice requires you to say more than you did last night?"

"Miss Walton," I replied, "to you, who know nothing of the difficult and hopeless position in which I stand, my conduct, I presume, seems most dishonorable and cowardly; yet I cannot say more than I said last night."

"You must."

"I can scarcely hope that what I then said will influence you, but if you will go to Mr. Blodgett and"—

"Does Mr. Blodgett know what you object to in Mr. Whitely?" you interrupted.

"Yes."

"I went to Mr. Blodgett this morning, and he told me that he knew of no reason why I should not marry Mr. Whitely."

"Then, Miss Walton," I answered, rising, "I cannot expect that you will be influenced by my opinion. I will withdraw what I said last night. Think of me as leniently as you can, for my purpose was honorable."

"But you ought to say more. You"—

"I cannot," I replied.

"You have no right to"—But here a servant entered, with a card.

"Dr. Hartzmann," you announced, when the man had gone, "I wrote Mr. Whitely yesterday afternoon, asking him to call this evening, with the intention of accepting his offer of marriage. He is now in the drawing-room, and unless you will have the fairness, the honesty, to explain what you meant, I shall tell him all that has occurred, and give him the opportunity to force you to speak."

"I shall only repeat to him, Miss Walton, what I have said to you."

You stood a moment looking at me, with a face blazing with indignation; then you exclaimed, "You at least owe it to him not to run away while I am gone!" and passed into the drawing-room.

You returned very soon, followed by Mr. Whitely.

"Dr. Hartzmann," you asked, "will you repeat what you said last night to me?"

"I advised you not to marry Mr. Whitely, Miss Walton."

"And you will not say why?" you demanded.

"I cannot."

"Mr. Whitely," you cried, "cannot you force him to speak?"

"Miss Walton," he replied suavely, and his very coolness in the strange condition made me feel that he was master of the situation, "I am as perplexed as you are at this extraordinary conduct in one who even now is eating bread from my hand. I have long since ceased to expect gratitude for benefits, but such malevolence surprises and grieves me, since I have never done Dr. Hartzmann any wrong, but, on the contrary, I have always befriended him."

"I have been in the employ of Mr. Whitely," I answered, "but every dollar he has paid me has been earned by my labor. I owe him no debt of gratitude that he does not owe me."

"You owe him the justice that every man owes another," you asserted indignantly. "To make vague charges behind one's back, and then refuse to be explicit, is a coward's and a slanderer's way of waging war."

"Miss Walton," I cried, "I should not have spoken, though God knows that my motive was only a wish to do you a service, and I would give my life to do as you ask!"

For an instant my earnestness seemed to sway you; indeed, I am convinced that this was so, since Mr. Whitely apparently had the same feeling, and spoke as if to neutralize my influence, saying to you: "Miss Walton, I firmly believe that Dr. Hartzmann's plea of honorable conduct is nothing but the ambush of a coward. But as he has been for two years in the most intimate and confidential position of private secretary to me, he may, through some error, have deluded himself into a conviction that gives a basis for his indefinite charges. I will not take advantage of the implied secrecy, and I say to him in your presence that if he has discovered anything which indicates that I have been either impure or criminal, I give him permission to speak."

Even in that moment of entanglement I could not but admire and marvel at the skill with which he had phrased his speech, so as to seem absolutely open, to slur me by innuendo, and yet avoid the risk of exposure. It left me helpless, and I could only say, "I have not charged Mr. Whitely with either impurity or criminality."

You turned to him and said, "This conduct is perfectly inexplicable."

"Except on one ground," he replied.

"Which is?" you questioned.

"That Dr. Hartzmann loves you," he answered.

"That is impossible!" you exclaimed.

"Not as impossible as for a man not to love you, Miss Walton," he averred.

"Tell Mr. Whitely how mistaken he is," you said to me.

I could only stand silent, and after waiting a little Mr. Whitely remarked, "You see!"

"It is incredible!" you protested. "You must deny it, Dr. Hartzmann!"

"I cannot, Miss Walton," I murmured, with bowed head.

"You love me?" you cried incredulously.

"I love you," I assented, and in spite of the circumstances it was happiness to say it to you.

You stood gazing at me in amazement, large-eyed as a startled deer. I wonder what your first words would have been to me if Mr. Whitely had not turned your mind into another channel by saying, "I do not think that we need search further for Dr. Hartzmann's motives in making his innuendoes."

"Miss Walton," I urged, "my love for you, far from making your faith in me less or my motive that of a rival, should convince you that I spoke only for your sake, since you yourself know that my love has been neither hopeful nor self-seeking."

I think you pitied me, for you answered gently, and all traces of the scorn and indignation you had shown just before were gone from your face and manner.

"Dr. Hartzmann," you said, "I cannot allow myself to listen to or weigh such indefinite imputations against Mr. Whitely. I will give you one week to explain or substantiate what you have implied; and unless within that time you do so, I shall accept the offer of marriage which he has honored me by making. Do not let me detain you further. Good-evening."

I passed out of the room a broken-hearted man, without strength enough to hold up my head, and hardly able in my weakness to crawl back to my study. As I sit and write, every breath brings with it the feeling that a knife is being thrust into my breast, and I am faint with the pain. But for this racking cough and burning fever I might have made a better fight, and have been able to think of some way of saving you. But even in my suffering I have reached one conclusion. To-morrow I shall go to Mr. Whitely and tell him that you must know the truth concerning the book, and that if he will not tell you I shall. I shall never be able to hold up my head again; but that is nothing, if I can but save you. Oh, my dearest love, the sacrifice of life, of honor, the meeting ignominy or death for your sake, will be nothing to me but hap

> [Transcriber's Note: The text ends in the middle of a word. The remainder of this page is missing in the original image and other available editions.]

XXV

January 10, 1895. This evening I have for the first time re-read this—I know not what to call it, for it is neither diary nor letter—the story of my love; and as I read, the singular sensation came over me that I was following, not my own thoughts and experiences, but those of another man. Five years ago, half mad with grief, and physically and nervously exhausted to the brink of a breakdown, I spent my evenings writing my thoughts, in the hope that the fatigue of the task would bring the sleep I sought in vain. Little I then wrote seems to me now, in my new life, what I could ever possibly have confided to paper, much less have felt. Yet here is my own handwriting to vouch for every word, and to tell me that the morbid chronicle is no other than my own. I cannot believe that mere years have brought so startling a mental change, and I therefore think that much of it is an expression, not of myself, but of the illness which put an end to my writing. If proof were needed of the many kinds of men each man contains, this manuscript of mine would furnish it; for the being I have read about this evening is no more the Donald Maitland of to-night than— Ah, well, to my task of telling what has wrought this change, since it must be written.

For a month I was confined to my bed with pneumonia, and the attack so weakened me that I did not leave my room for five weeks more. During that time Mrs. Blodgett's kindness was constant, and her face is the only memory that stands out from the hours of my acute torture. While I was convalescing, she came once, and sometimes twice, each day, bringing me flowers, fruit, jellies, wines, and whatever else her love could suggest. It was amusing to see her domineer over the doctor, trained nurse, and landlady, and I soon learned to whom to make my pleas for extra liberty or special privileges. No request, however whimsical, seemed too much for her affection, though my demands were unceasing, in the selfishness of my invalidism. Only one thing I dared not ask her, and that was not from fear that it would be refused, but from cowardice. I longed to have her speak of you, but during those weeks she never mentioned your name.

The day before Mrs. Blodgett left town she took me for my first airing in her carriage, and told me that she was leaving a man and horses in town for a month longer in order that I should have a daily drive. "Mr. Blodgett really needs a carriage more in the summer than he does in the winter, but he never will consent to let me leave one for him, so I've used you as an excuse," was the way she explained her kindness. "By the end of the month I hope you will be well enough to come up and make us a visit in the Berkshires, for the change will be the very best thing for you."

"I hope to be at work again by that time," I said.

"You are not to see pen or paper till the first of October!" she ordered; and when I only shook my head, she continued, "For three years you've been overworking yourself, and now the doctor says you must take a long rest, and I'm going to see that you have it."

"You mean to be good to me, Mrs. Blodgett," I sighed, "but if you knew my situation, you would understand that I must get to work again as soon as possible."

"I don't care about your situation," she sniffed contemptuously, "and I do care about your health. I shall insist that you come up to My Fancy, if I have to come back to the city to bring you; and when I once get you there, I shan't let you go away till I choose."

Loving my tyrant, I did not protest further, though firm in my own mind as to my duty. As it turned out, I need not have denied her, for the end of the month found me with but little added strength; and though I tried to work two or three times, I was forced to abandon the attempts without accomplishing anything. My wonder is that I gained strength at all, in my discouragement over the loss of Mr. Whitely's work, my three months' idleness, the heavy doctor's bills, and the steadily accruing interest on the debt.

On the 21st of June Mr. Blodgett came to see me, as indeed he had done daily since Mrs. Blodgett left town.

"The boss writes," he announced, "ordering me to come up to-day, and directing that before I leave New York I am to do forty-seven things, ranging in importance from buying her the last novels to matching some white"—he looked at his letter, and spelled out—"'f-l-o-s-s' as per sample inclosed. I haven't time to do more than forty-five, and I'm afraid I'll never hear the last of the remaining two unless you'll save me."

"How?"

"Well, three times in her letter she tells me that I've got to bring you, the last time as good as saying that my life won't be an insurable risk if I don't. Since she puts so much stress on your presence, it's just possible that if I fill that order she'll forget the rest."

"I would go, Mr. Blodgett, but"—

"Oh, I understand all that," he interrupted. "Of course, if you stay in the cool fresh air of the city, you won't run any risk of the malaria the Berkshires are full of; I know the New York markets have peas as large and firm as bullets, while those in our garden are poor little shriveled affairs hardly worth the trouble of eating; our roads are not Belgian blocks, but only soft dirt, and we haven't got a decent flagged sidewalk within ten miles of My Fancy. I understand perfectly that you'll get well faster here, and so get to work sooner; but all the same, just as a favor, you might pull me out of this scrape."

I need not say I had to yield, and together we took the afternoon express. On the train we found Mr. Whitely,—as great a surprise, apparently, to Mr. Blodgett as it was to me.

"Hello!" exclaimed the banker. "Where are you bound for?"

"I presume for the same destination you are," Mr. Whitely replied. "I am going up to see Miss Walton, and if Mrs. Blodgett cannot give me a night's hospitality, I shall go to the hotel."

"Plenty of room at My Fancy, and I'll guarantee your welcome," promised Mr. Blodgett pleasantly. "Here's the doctor going up for a bit of nursing."

Much to my surprise, my former employer entered the compartment, and, offering me his hand, sat down by the lounge I was stretched upon. "You've had a serious illness," he remarked, with a bland attempt at sympathy.

I only nodded my head.

"I hope you will recover quickly, for you are needed in the office," he went on.

I could not have been more surprised if he had struck me, though I did not let it appear in my face.

"Whitely's been trying to go it alone on his editorials, and the papers have all been laughing at him," chuckled Mr. Blodgett. "Just read us your famous one, Whitely,—that one about The Tendency of Modern Art, with the original Hebrew from Solomon you put in."

I saw my employer redden, and in pity for his embarrassment I said, "I do not think I shall ever come back to the office, Mr. Whitely."

"Why not?" he exclaimed. "You committed an unwise action, but business is business, and I see no cause why we need let a single mistake terminate a relation mutually profitable."

"I have learned the lesson that one cannot sell one's honesty without wronging other people, and I shall never do it again."

"This is purely sentimental"—he began.

Mr. Blodgett, however, interrupted by saying, "Now don't go to exciting the doctor, for he's to sleep on the trip. Besides, I've got something in mind better than the job he's had under you, Whitely. Come and have a smoke, and leave him to nap a bit."

They left me, and I set to puzzling over many questions: how you would greet me at My Fancy; how you would welcome Mr. Whitely; what was the meaning of his friendliness towards me; and what new kindness Mr. Blodgett had in store for me. Finally I fell asleep, to be awakened only when we reached our destination.

Agnes met us at the station, and at the house Mrs. Blodgett gave me the warmest of welcomes, but not till I came downstairs before dinner did you and I meet. Your greeting was formal, yet courteous and gracious as of old, almost making me question if our last two interviews could be realities.

Before the dinner was finished Mrs. Blodgett ordered me to the divan on the veranda, and sent dessert and fruit out to me. You all joined me when the moment came for coffee and cigars; but the evening was cloudy and rather breezy, and presently Mrs. Blodgett said it was too cold for her, and suggested a game of whist indoors. "You must stay out here," she told me, "but if you feel cool be sure to use the shawl."

You turned and said to Mr. Whitely, "You will play, I hope?" and he assented so eagerly that it was all I could do to keep from laughing outright when you continued, "Agnes and Mr. Whitely will make your table, Mrs. Blodgett, so I will stay here and watch the clouds." The whole thing was so palpably with an object that I felt at once that you wished to see me alone, to learn if I had anything more to say concerning Mr. Whitely; and as I realized this, I braced myself for the coming ordeal.

For a few moments you stood watching the gathering storm, and then took a chair by the divan on which I lay.

"Are you too honorable," you began,—and though I could not see your face in the darkness, your voice told me you were excited,—"to pardon dishonorable conduct in others? For I have come to beg of you forgiveness for a wrong."

"Of me, Miss Walton?"

"Last April," you went on, "Mrs. Blodgett brought me a book and asked me to read it. A few paragraphs revealed to me that it was something written by an old friend of mine. After reading a little further, I realized for the first time that I was violating a confidence. Yet though I knew this, and struggled to close the book, I could not, but read it to the end. Can you forgive me?"

"Oh, Miss Walton!" I protested. "Why ask forgiveness of me? What is your act compared to the wrong"—

"Hush, Don," you said gently, and your use of my name, so long unheard, told me in a word that the feeling of our childhood days was come again. "Tell me you forgive me!" you entreated.

"I am not the one to forgive, Maizie."

"I did wrong, and I ask your pardon," you begged humbly. "Yet I'm not sorry in the least, and I should do it again," you instantly added, laughing merrily at your own perverseness. Then in a moment you were serious again, saying, "I never received the letters or the photograph, Donald. My uncle confesses that he put them in the fire." And before I could speak, a new thought seized you, for you continued sadly, "I shall never forgive myself for my harshness and cruelty when you were so ill."

"That is nothing," I replied, "since all our misunderstandings are gone. Why, even my debt, Maizie, ceases now to be a burden; in the future it will be only a joy to work."

"Donald!" you exclaimed. "You don't suppose I shall let you pay me another cent!"

"I must."

"But I am rich," you protested. "The money is nothing to me. You shall not ruin your career to pay it. I scorn myself when I think that I refused to see you that night, and so lost my only chance of saving you from what followed. My cowardice, my wicked cowardice! It drove you to death's door by overwork, to give me wealth I do not know how to spend. You parted with your library that I might let money lie idle in bank. I forced you to sell your book—your fame—to that thief. Oh, Donald, think of the wrong it has done already, and don't make it do greater!"

"Maizie, you do not understand"—

"I understand it all," you interrupted. "You must not—you shall not—I won't take it—I"—

"For his sake!"

"But I love him, too!" you pleaded. "Don't you see, Donald, that it was never the money,—that was nothing; but they told me his love—and yours, for they said you had known all the time—was only pretense, a method by which you might continue to rob me. And I came to believe it,—though I should have known better,—because, since you never wrote, it seemed to me you had both dropped me out of your thoughts as soon as you could no longer plunder me. Even then, scorning you,—like you in your feeling over my neglect of your letters,—I could not help loving you, for those Paris and Tyrol days were the happiest I have ever known; and though I knew, Don, that I ought to forget you, as I believed you had forgotten me, I could not do so. I have never dared to speak in public of either of you, for fear I should break down. Try as I might, I could not help loving you both as I have never loved any one else. That I turned you away from my house was because I did not dare to meet you,—I knew I could not control myself. After the man took the message, I sobbed over having to insult you by sending it by a servant. But for my want of courage—had I seen you as I ought—If I had only understood, as your journal has made me,—had only known that my name was on his lips when he died! No money could pay for what he gave to me. Could he ask me now for twice the sum, it would be my pleasure to give it to him, for I love him dearly, and"—

"If you love him, Maizie, you will let me clear his name as far as lies within my power."

For an instant you were silent, and then said softly, "You are right, Donald, we will clear his name."

I took your hand and touched it to my lips. "To hear you speak of him"—I could go no further, in my emotion.

There was a pause before you asked, "Donald, do you remember our talk here last autumn?"

"Every word."

You laughed gayly. "I want you to know, sir," you asserted, with a pretense of defiance, "that I don't believe in love, because I have never found any that was wholly free from self-indulgence or self-interest. And I still think"—

Just then Mrs. Blodgett joined us, and inquired, "Have you told Rudolph, Maizie?"

"Yes."

"I went to see how you were the moment I heard of your illness," she said, with a certain challenge in her voice, "and I found that book lying on your desk just where you stopped writing from weakness. I read it, and I took it to Maizie."

"It was kismet, I suppose," was all I could say, too happy to think of criticism, and instantly her manner changed and she wiped her eyes.

"I had to do it," she sobbed.

"You have been too good to me," I answered, rising and taking her hand.

"There, there," she continued, steadying herself. "I didn't come out to behave like this, but to tell you to go to bed at once. I'm going to your room to see that everything is right for our invalid, but don't you delay a minute after I'm gone," and she disappeared through the doorway.

I turned to you and held out my hand, bidding you, "Good-night, Maizie," and you took it, and replied, "Goodnight, Don." Then suddenly you leaned forward, and, kissing my forehead, added, "God keep you safe for me, my darling."

I took you in my arms, and gave you back your kiss twofold, while saying, "Good-night, my love."

XXVI

A man does not willingly spread on paper the sweetest and tenderest moments of his life. When half crazed with grief and illness I might express my suffering, much as, in physical pain, some groan aloud; but the deepest happiness is silent, for it is too great to be told. And lest, my dears, you think me even less manly than I am, I choose to add here the reason for my writing the last few pages of this story of my love, that if you ever read it you may know the motive which made me tell what till to-night I have kept locked in my heart.

This evening the dearest woman in the world came to me, as I sat at my desk in the old library, and asked, "Are you busy, Donald?"

"I am reading the one hundred and forty-seventh complimentary review of my History of the Moors, and I am so sick of sweets that your interruption comes as an unalloyed pleasure."

"Am I bitter or acid?" she asked, leaning over my shoulder and arranging my hair, which is one of her ways of pleasing me.

"You are my exact opposite," I said gravely.

"How uncomplimentary you are!" she cried, with a pretense of anger in her voice.

"An historian must tell the truth now and then, for variety's sake."

"Then tell me if you are too engaged to spare me a minute. Any other time will do."

"You are seriously mistaken, because no other time will do. And nothing about me is ever engaged, as regards you, except my affections, and they are permanently so."

"I've come to ask a great favor of you."

"Out of the question; but you may tell me what it is."

"Ah, Donald, say you will grant it before I tell you?"

"Concealment bespeaks a guilty conscience."

"But sometimes you are so funny and obstinate about things!"

"That is what Mr. Whitely used to say."

"Don't mention that wretch's name to me! To think of that miserable little Western college making him an LL. D. because of your book!"

"Never mind, Maizie; here's a letter I received an hour ago from Jastrow, which tells me the University of Leipzig is going to give me a degree."

"That he should steal your fame!"

"My Moor is five times the chap my Turk was."

"But you might have had both!"

"And gone without you? Don't fret over it, my darling."

"I can't help"—

She always ends this vein by abusing herself, which I wouldn't allow another human being to do, and which I don't like to hear, so I interrupted: "Jastrow says he'll come over in March to visit us, and threatens to bring the manuscript of his whole seventeen volumes, for me to take a final look at it before he sends it to press."

"The dear old thing!" she said tenderly. "I love him so for what he was to you that I believe I shall welcome him with a kiss."

"Why make the rest of his life unhappy?"

"Is that the way it affects you?"

"Woman is born illogical, and even the cleverest of her sex cannot entirely overcome the taint. After you give me a kiss I bear in mind that I am to have another, and that makes me very happy. But if you kiss Jastrow, the poor fellow will go back to Germany and pine away into his grave. Even his fifty-two dialects will not satisfy him after your labial."

"Oh, you silly!" she exclaimed; but, my dears, I think she is really, in her secret heart, fond of silliness, for she leaned over and—There, I'll stop being what she called me.

"We'll give him a great reception," she continued, "and have every one worth knowing to meet him."

"He is the shyest of beings."

"How books and learning do refine men!" she said.

"I am afraid they do make weaklings of us."

"Will you never get over the idea that you are weak?" she cried; for it is one of her pet superstitions that I am not.

"You'll frighten me out of it if you speak like that."

"You are—well—that is really what I came to ask for. Just to please your own wife, you will, Donald, won't you?"

"The distinction between 'will' and 'won't' is clearly set forth in a somewhat well-known song concerning a spider and a fly."

"Oh, you bad boy!"

"Adsum."

"I'm really serious."

"I never was less so."

"I should not have become your wife if I had dreamed you would be such a brute!"

"You'll please remember that I never asked you to marry me."

She laughed deliciously over the insult, and after that I could not resist her.

"You have," I said, "a bundle in your left hand, wrapped in tissue paper and tied with a blue ribbon, which you sedulously keep from my sight, but of which I caught a glimpse as you entered."

"And you've known it all this time! Perhaps you know too what I want?"

"Last spring," I answered, "I knocked at the door of your morning-room twice, and receiving no response, I went in, to find you reading something that you instantly hid from sight. There were on the lounge, I remember, a sheet of tissue paper and a blue ribbon. I suspect a connection."

"Well?"

"My theory is that you have some really improper book wrapped in the paper, and that is why you so guiltily hide it from me."

"Oh, Donald, it gives me such happiness to read it!"

"That was the reason I asked you why you had tears in your eyes, when I surprised you that day. Your happiness was most enviable!"

"Men never understand women!"

"Deo gratias."

"But I love it."

"I don't like to hear you express such sentiments for so erotic a book."

"Oh, don't apply such a word to it!" she cried, in a pained voice.

"A word," I explained, "taken from the Greek *erotikos*, which is derived from *erao*, meaning 'I love passionately.' It is singularly descriptive, Maizie."

"If it means that, I like it, but I thought you were insulting my book."

"Almost five years ago," I remarked, "a volume was stolen from my room, which I have never since been able to recover. Now a woman of excessive honesty calmly calls it hers."

"You know you don't want it."

"I want it very much."

"Really?"

"To put it in the fire."

"Don!"

"Once upon a time a most bewitching woman wrote a story, and in a vain moment her husband asked her to give it to him. She"—

"But, my darling, it was so foolish that I had to burn it up. Think of my making the heroine marry that creature!"

"Since you married the poor chap to the other girl, there was no other ending possible. If the book were only in existence, I think Agnes and her husband would enjoy reading it almost as much as I should."

"How silly I was! But at least the book made you write the ending which prevented me from accepting him that winter. What a lot of trouble I gave my poor dear!"

"I met the 'poor dear' yesterday, looking very old and unhappy despite his LL. D."

"Oh, you idiot!" she laughed. And she must like imbeciles, too, for—well, I'm not going to tell even you how I know that she's fond of idiots.

"Why do you suppose he's unhappy?" she asked.

"My theory is that he's miserable because he lost—lost me."

"I'm so glad he is!" joyously asserted the tenderest of women.

"Nevertheless," I resumed, "it was a book I should have valued as much as you do that one in tissue paper, and you ought not to have burned it."

"I am very sorry I did, Donald, since you would really have liked it," she said, wistfully and sorrowfully. "I should have thought of your feelings, and not of mine."

This is a mood I cannot withstand. "Dear heart," I responded, "I have you, and all the books in the world are not worth a breath in comparison. What favor do you want me to do?"

"To write a sort of last chapter—an ending, you know—telling about—about the rest."

"Have you forgotten it?"

"I? Never! I couldn't. But I want to have it all in the book, so that when Foster and Mai are older they can read it."

"I have no intention of sharing, even with our children, my under-the-rose idyl with the loveliest of girls. And when the children are older, they'll be far more interested in their own heart secrets than they are in ours."

"Still, dear," she pleaded, "they may hear from others some unkind and perverted allusions to our story; for you know what foolish things were said at the time of our marriage."

"If I remember rightly, some one—was it my mother or Mr. Whitely?"—

"Both," she answered.

"—spread it abroad that I had trapped an heiress into marriage by means of an alias."

"Wasn't it a delicious version!" she laughed merrily. "But no matter what's ever tattled in the future, if Foster and Mai have your journal, they will always understand it."

"Maizie," I urged, "if you let those imps of mischief read of our childish doings in this old library, they'll either finish painting the plates in Kingsborough, or burn the house down in trying to realize an Inca of Peru at the stake."

"But I won't read them those parts," she promised; "especially if you write a nice ending, which they'll like."

"Won't it do to add just a paragraph, saying that our fairy godmamma found and gave you the journal, and that then we 'lived happily ever after'?"

"No, Donald," she begged. "I want the whole story, to match the rest."

"Five years ago I knew the saddest and most dejected of fellows, whose misery was so great that he wailed it out on paper. But now I know only the happiest of mortals, and he cannot write in the lugubrious tone of yore—unless a lady of his acquaintance will banish him from her presence or do something else equally joy-destroying."

"Are you trying to bribe me into giving you a rest from my presence for a time?"

"Undoubtedly," I assented. "It's a fearful strain to live up to you, and it is beginning to tell on me."

"If I didn't know you were teasing, I should really be hurt. But I should like to ask you one thing."

"And that is?"

"In your journal—well—of course I know that you were—that I am not—that your love made you think me what I never was in the least, Donald," she faltered, "but still, perhaps—Do you remember what Mr. Blodgett said about his not giving Mrs. Blodgett for ten of the women he—? I hope you like my reality as much as your ideal."

"Haven't you changed your idea of me, Maizie?"

"Oh yes."

"And therefore you don't love me as much?"

"But that's different, Donald," she observed seriously.

"How?"

"Why, you treated me so strangely that, inevitably, I didn't know what you were like; and though you interested me very much, and though your journal brought back my old love for you, still, what I did was more in pity and admiration and reparation than—and so I could fall deeper in love. While you, being so much in love already, and with such a totally different woman"—

"Only went from bad to worse," I groaned. "Yes, I own up. My sin is one of the lowest man can commit. I have fallen in love with a married woman. And the strange thing about it is that you are not jealous of her! Indeed, I really believe that you are magnanimous enough to love her too, though it's natural you should not like her as much as you do some others. But next August I'll leave her and go to India to study for my new book."

"The married woman will go too," she predicted calmly.

"I shouldn't dare risk her among those hill tribes."

"And she won't risk you where it isn't safe for her to go."

"I was only thinking of your lovely complexion," I explained.

"Old mahogany is very fashionable," she laughed.

"Can nothing make you stay at home?" I asked beseechingly.

"I wonder if there ever was a husband who did not love to tease his wife?"

"The divorce courts have records of many such unloving wretches."

"What I want," she told me, returning to her wish, "is to have you take it up just where you left off. Tell about your pneumonia, and how Mrs. Blodgett found your journal, but didn't dare give it to me till the doctor was certain you would recover; and then tell of my sending you flowers and jellies and everything I could think of, by her, to help you get well. How"—

"I should have eaten twice as much and recovered much more quickly if she had only let me know from whom they really came," I interjected in an aggrieved tone.

"And tell how I wouldn't listen to that scoundrel till you should have a chance to justify yourself; how, the moment I had read your diary, I wrote and rejected him, and would not see him when he called; how he would not accept his dismissal, but followed me to the country; tell how dreadfully in the way he was that evening, till Mrs. Blodgett and Agnes and I trapped him into a game of whist"—

"You Machiavellis!"

"Tell all about my confession, and how we all spoiled you for those months at My Fancy. Oh, weren't they lovely, Donald?"

"I thought so then."

"But not now?"

"A gooseberry is good till you taste a strawberry. There was a good deal too much gooseberry, as I remember."

"Then tell how the papers and people chattered about your assuming your true name; and how they gabbled when we were married,—and how, on our wedding day, we endowed the hospital ward"—

"Haven't you made a slip in the pronoun?"

"I'll box your ears if you even suggest it again; half of the money was what you earned—endowed the hospital ward in memory of *our* dear father, and how happy we've been since."

"You've made a mistake in the last pronoun, I'm certain."

"You will write it to please me, Donald?"

"Oh, Maizie, I can't. It's all too dear to me."

"Please, Don, try?"

"But"—

She interrupted my protest. "Donald," she said, the tenderness in her face and voice softening her words, "before knowing that I loved you, you insisted that debt must be paid. Won't you pay me now, dear?"

"I don't merely owe you money, Maizie!" I cried. "I owe you everything, and I'm a brute to the most generous of women. Give me the book, dear heart."

"You'll make it nice, like the rest, won't you?" she begged.

"I'll try." And then I laughingly added, "Maizie, you still have the technical part of story-telling to learn."

"How?"

"I can't write all you wish and make it symmetrical. In the first place, we don't want to spend so much time on Whitely as to give him a fictitious value; and next, to be artistic, we must end with our good-night that evening."

"Well, that will do, if you'll only tell it nicely."

And that, my dears, is why I write again of those old days, so distant now in time and mood. What is told here is shared with you only to please my love, and I ask of you that it shall be a confidence. And of Another I beg that each of you in time may find a love as strong as that told here; that each may be as true and noble as your mother, and as happy as your father.

Good-night, my children. Good-night, my love. May God be as good to you as he has been to me.

Milton Keynes UK
Ingram Content Group UK Ltd.
UKHW031146311024
450535UK00004B/137

9 789362 922670